CAREER RESOURCES FOR A LI᷈ ᷈ ᷈ ᷈ ᷈ ᷈ ᷈ ᷈

Solo by Choice, The Companion Guide: 34 Questions That Could Transform Your Legal Career
By Carolyn Elefant $30/134pages (2011)

Solo By Choice 2011/2012 Edition: How to Be the Lawyer You Always Wanted to Be
By Carolyn Elefant $45/316 pages (2nd Ed., 2011)

Should You Really Be a Lawyer? The Guide to Smart Career Choices Before, During & After Law School
By Deborah Schneider & Gary Belsky $25/276 pages (2nd Ed., 2010)

The View From the First Chair: What Every Trial Lawyer Really Needs to Know
By Martin L. Grayson $45 /170 pages (2009)

Lawyers at Midlife: Laying the Groundwork for the Road Ahead
By Michael Long with John Clyde & Pat Funk $35 /224 pages (2008)

What Can You Do With a Law Degree? Career Alternatives Inside, Outside & Around the Law
By Deborah Arron $30 /352 pages (5th Ed., 2004)

Should You Marry a Lawyer? A Couple's Guide to Balancing Work, Love & Ambition
By Fiona Travis, Ph.D. $19 /168 pages (2004)

Running From the Law: Why Good Lawyers Are Getting Out of the Legal Profession
By Deborah Arron $17 /192 pages (3rd Ed., 2003)

Available (with free shipping) from LawyerAvenue Press at www.LawyerAvenue.com.

SOLO BY CHOICE
The Companion Guide

34 Questions
That Could Transform
Your Legal Career

Published by LawyerAvenue Press and its imprint, DecisionBooks.

Interior design by Elizabeth Watson
Cover design by Rose Michelle Taverniti

Volume discounts available from LawyerAvenue Press.
Email to editor@LawyerAvenue.com or write to Avenue Productions,
4701 SW Admiral Way #278, Seattle WA 98116

Author Carolyn Elefant offers keynote addresses, webinars,
presentations, and workshops. For more information, contact the
author at her Web site: www.MyShingle.com.

Library of Congress Cataloging-in-Publication Data

Elefant, Carolyn.
  Solo by choice, the companion guide : 34 questions that could
transform your legal career / [Carolyn Elefant].
      p. cm.
  A companion to: Solo by choice 2011-2012. 2nd ed. 2011.
  ISBN 978-0-940675-64-3 (pbk.)
  1. Solo law practice--United States. 2. Practice of law--United
States. 3. Law offices--United States. 4. Lawyers--United States. I.
Elefant, Carolyn. Solo by choice 2011-2012. II. Title.
  KF300.E423 2011
  340.023'73--dc23
                              2011024923

Printed in the United States of America

PREFACE

Once upon a time, our profession relied on each other to train and pass knowledge down to the next generation. Large firms groomed their young associates for partnership, while solos trained apprentices to eventually join or take over their practices.

Now, fast forward to the 21st Century.

Today, much of the lawyer-to-lawyer mentorship and sense of obligation to prepare younger lawyers for practice has been eviscerated for two reasons: first, as the numbers of lawyers increase and jobs decline, the drive to hoard cases and increase profits has overshadowed the desire to improve the legal profession. And second, mentorship has gone commercial, with paid experts and coaches charging for the advice that lawyers once rendered for free.

In spite of these changes, our profession's great tradition of benevolence and mentorship still thrives in the solo community. Just ask any solo how they got their start. Invariably, they will attribute their success to a more experienced solo—a former employer or a colleague in the same town—who offered guidance or who referred cases during the early days of their practice. It's even truer today . . . thanks to the Internet. From listservs (especially Solosez!) to solo blogs, LinkedIn groups, and Facebook communities, good, solid advice on starting a firm, dealing with clients, or handling the financial pressures of solo practice is flowing abundantly . . . and freely.

This book, this *Companion Guide* to my other work, *Solo by Choice*, is an outgrowth of this spirit of solo-to-solo sharing.

From first page to last, this book introduces you to some 50 solo practitioners from across the country—all ages, all types, all at different stages of their law careers—who generously volunteered their insight, advice, first-hand lessons, and inspiration and encouragement to help new and prospective solos like you. Their testimony—in their own words—reinforces what I've always known to be true: there are as many ways to start a law firm as there are solos, and that each of us brings our own unique talents, personalities, and passions to our respective practices. It's certainly true of the solos quoted here. Yet despite the diverse opinions and approaches to practice that you find here, several common themes ring loud and clear: an acknowledgement and cheerful willingness to accept the personal sacrifices that come with starting a law firm; a deep gratitude for the support of families and trusted friends; and, most of all, an indefatigable optimism about future opportunities.

In short, I believe the lawyers featured here capture the true spirit of what it means to be a solo practitioner.

—Carolyn Elefant, August, 2011

PART ONE

In the Beginning 9

....

1. Is there a solo type? *10*

2. Why did you decide to solo? *12*

3. What did you know about solo
practice before you began? *16*

4. How did you explain your decision
to colleagues? *18*

5. Who was the most supportive of
your decision? *20*

6. What are your sharpest memories
of starting out? *21*

7. What sacrifices did you make
to solo? *24*

8. How did you create a revenue
stream in the beginning? *26*

PART TWO

A Day in the Life 31

....

9. What role does a spouse/partner
play in a solo's success? *32*

10. How do you balance parenting
with a solo practice? *35*

11. What practice skills were you least
prepared for? *36*

12. What was your most difficult client
experience, and what you did learn? . . . *38*

13. Should new lawyers open a
solo practice? *42*

14. What was your biggest goof, and
what did it teach you? *47*

15. What important issues do new
solos face? *48*

16. What role does risk play in a
solo practice? *50*

17. What are the biggest challenges
when you're the boss? *53*

18. What do you like/dislike about
the autonomy of solo practice? *55*

19. What frustrations are solos likely
to experience? *57*

20. What role do mentors play in
your practice? *58*

21. What role do people skills play in
a solo's success? *60*

PART THREE

The Business of Solo'ing 63

22. What business skills are essential for a solo? *64*

23. How do you market your legal practice? *65*

24. What marketing advice do you have for new solos?. *67*

25. What financial issues loom in the first year? *71*

26. Can you solo on a shoestring budget? . *74*

27. What about job security?. *76*

28. How important is a business plan?. . . . *78*

29. What would you tell new solos about malpractice insurance? *81*

30. What role does social media play in marketing your practice and building relationships? *84*

31. What are you doing to stay profitable? . *86*

32. What is your Plan B if things don't work out?. *88*

PART FOUR

Reflections 89

33. Would you still solo given what you've learned? *90*

34. Where do you see the practice of law, and solo'ing, headed?. *92*

PART FIVE

Solos by Choice:
The Expanded Profiles 95

1. Kevin Afghani (Class of 2004). *96*

2. Gina Bongiovi (Class of 2007) *98*

3. Bruce Cameron (Class of 2007) *100*

4. Lynda L. Hinkle (Class of 2009) *103*

5. Mitchell J. Matorin (Class of 1993)   *105*

6. Kara O'Donnell (Class of 1995). *107*

7. Paul Scott (Class of 2008) *109*

8. Jan M. Tamanini (Class of 1984) *111*

9. Mark Tanney (Class of 1998) *113*

Solos by Choice:
The Complete List of
Companion Guide Contributors 117

APPENDIX

The Case for Solo Practice 127

PART ONE:
In the Beginning

1. Is there a solo type?

2. Why did you decide to solo?

3. What did you know about solo practice before you began?

4. How did you explain your decision to colleagues?

5. Who was the most supportive of your decision?

6. What are your sharpest memories of starting out?

7. What sacrifices did you make to solo?

8. How did you create a revenue stream in the beginning?

Introduction

I t's been said that the hardest part of any journey is the first step. Nothing could be more true than for the journey towards starting one's own law firm. For lawyers who never expected or even desired to solo, that first step asks that you get beyond the misconceptions of solo practice; and for the lawyers who wanted to solo from the outset, the first step asks that you face an assortment of financial, economic, and psychological challenges that don't have be faced by lawyers going in-house, into firms, or into government.

In the pages that follow, we raise 34 important questions that could transform your legal career. But it is the first eight questions that I believe go to the heart of what so many new and prospective solos think about. Fortunately you will find assurance here that you do have what it takes to start a firm, and that while the early years will involve some sacrifice, the price to be paid is more than worthwhile for the memories of those exciting first days of practice . . . and more importantly, for everything that you create afterward.

It's my hope that the insight and advice found here will give you just enough of a push to take the first step to solo practice.

1. Is there a solo type?

"Some people excel in a BigLaw environment, others in a more structured government or in-house environment. A solo type has a high tolerance for risk, a high degree of self-reliance, and the resourcefulness to figure things out on one's own. Going solo also means being self-confident in one's work product and the ability to develop business." —**Kevin Afghani (class of 2004)**

"I see solos as the legal world's entrepreneur; someone who has replaced thinking like an employee with thinking as an employer. The only real difference between solos and non-solos is the solo's willingness to trade job security for the freedom to control their practice. In my experience, solos are willing to innovate, to question, to think differently about old problems, to be imaginative, and to be willing to fail."
—**Bruce Cameron (class of 2007)**

"Yes, there is a solo type. You have to be very self-motivated and reasonably organized. Otherwise, you will lose client trust or waste a lot of time."
—**Jeffrey G. Neu (class of 2006)**

"You have to be the type who wants to solo. Sustaining a solo practice takes a lot of discipline and active participation. If you're not decisive, or adept at working alone in an efficient manner, or disciplined to enough to set and follow schedules and deadlines, your [solo practice] probably won't succeed." —**Adam Neufer (class of 2009)**

"Yes, there is a solo type. They're the ones who don't take crap from some stuffed shirt who tells them that the ABC Corp. file is more important than their kid's ballgame or their daughter's recital. Those who think ABC's file is more important can stay in the legal factories and blow their brains out at 50." —**Marc W. Matheny (class of 1980)**

1. Is there a solo type?

"No, I do not think there is a specific type of person who is cut out to be a solo. People of all personalities are solo attorneys. [But if there is a solo type], it is the person who wants to run a business, and to live a happy life that he [or she] has some control over."
—**Paul Scott (class of 2008)**

"I'm not sure if there is a solo 'type', but a big requirement is the ability to do things for oneself —typing, taking calls, scheduling clients, billing, etc., in addition to your own attorney work. If you absolutely hate doing all that, you're not the solo 'type.'" —**Ubong Akpan (class of 2003)**

"I think there are traits that make going solo easier: a willingness to accept risk, a fondness for multi-tasking between operating a small business and practicing law, and a willingness to self-promote. But I also think there are many 'types' that share these and other solo traits."
– **Cailie A. Currin (class of 1988)**

"One really important thing about being solo is disciplining yourself to do what you have to within the time you have to do it. There's no one looking over your shoulder or e-mailing you to ask how you're progressing with a matter. So, if you're the type of person who needs constant poking to get work done, perhaps solo practice isn't right for you." —**Jan M. Tamanini (class of 1984)**

"The successful solo must have self-discipline! You don't have a supervisor breathing down your neck or a time card to punch. No one is taking issue with your billable hour quota, and you don't have a paycheck direct-deposited to your account every two weeks. You have to manage your time, manage your caseload, make your own schedule, and handle all the administrative stuff,

Are you the solo type?

After giving careful thought to your motives for solo'ing, you still need to consider whether solo practice suits your personality and temperament. Consider:

Do you crave independence? The most satisfied solos prefer to operate without affiliation to a larger controlling unit, and don't require others for guidance in conducting their business.

Are you comfortable wearing many hats? Successful solos act as project manager, office manager, HR director, business manager, strategic planner, VP for business development, and general worker bee, all of which can consume as much as half your day.

Are you enterprising? The most successful solos have a talent for spotting opportunities and taking advantage of them. For them, networking is a regular and enjoyable part of every week, and they don't rely on telephone ads to keep their operation afloat.

What is your tolerance for risk? There's the possibility of great payoffs, and then you might run into days (even weeks) without billables. In order to experience satisfaction as a solo, you must be comfortable with the part of you that is willing to take a leap of faith . . . or willing to diversify your practice.

Are you a self-starter? Successful solos don't need someone looking over their shoulders; they're motivated to do what needs to be done.

Are you resourceful? The most successful solos are good at finding answers quickly, and are unafraid of asking questions, requesting input, and seeking help.

too. Gradually you will find people to whom you can delegate certain tasks, but you are still the person who makes sure it's all done right. Some people just don't have the desire to shoulder that much responsibility. And that's okay. Just be honest with yourself about your personality and your motivations, or you'll be a miserable square peg in a round hole."
—**Gina Bongiovi (class of 2007)**

"I think the key here is one's strong desire to be a solo. If you have that, you have a good chance to succeed. Beyond that, of course it helps to be tech-savvy, socially outgoing, and competent in the substantive law. But the key is your desire to be solo." —**Mark Tanney (class of 1998)**

"I don't know if there is a solo type, but there are definitely a few types that are not solo types. People who expect to swap one paycheck for another—that is, who think of themselves as employees instead of as owners and managers of a business—aren't going to do well. Salaried employees earn so much a week or so much a month, but solo practitioners have to think of earning so much a quarter or so much a year. A person who expects to take $X out of his or her firm every month isn't going to be happy, but one who has a sensible plan to earn $12X every year, and then carries out that plan, likely will be."
—**Dean N. Alterman (class of 1989)**

"I got tired of the hours, the commute, and not getting compensated for the amount of business I was bringing in. I was among the top five in business generation, but not anywhere near the top five in compensation!"
—**Walter D. James III (class of 1987)**

"The main reason I decided to solo was the birth of my first child, and the desire to devote more time to my family. I also consider myself an entrepreneur, and enjoy controlling the structure of my practice, scheduling my own days, and not being held back by the conventional structures of a traditional law practice."
—**Stephanie Kimbro (class of 2003)**

"The major factor [in deciding to solo] was in wanting to stay home with my children. Being a solo has worked out wonderfully by allowing me to spend most of my time with them."
—**Sarah White (class of 2002)**

"In my second year of law school, one of my professors described the typical life of a new attorney: it was the polar opposite of what I had attended law school to become. From then on, I knew I wanted to solo. I couldn't imagine toiling away four years of a part-time law program while working full or part-time, only to lose some of the freedom I'd enjoyed before enrolling in law school." —**Gina Bongiovi (class of 2007)**

"All through law school, bar study, and post-bar, I networked, volunteered, interned, worked contract work . . . and still there were no jobs. One month away from personal bankruptcy, I thought I might have it easier finding clients than finding a job. I was right. With only [modest] financial resources, I quickly built the knowledge base and experience through smart planning,

hard work, and with the help of wonderful colleagues."
—**Eric P. Ganci (class of 2008)**

"Why solo? My family is full of entrepreneurs, and throughout high school, college, and law school, I was self-employed. My personality has never allowed me to work for any companies or organizations, so I knew in law school that I would be going solo. Beyond that, I wanted to solo for the usual reasons: the ability to make my own schedule, the power of controlling my job security and destiny, the benefit of not having a promotional ceiling, the rewards of being in business for yourself, etc."
—**Scott Wolfe (class of 2005)**

"I wanted to sink or swim on my own. Do things in my own fashion rather than abide by the interminable partnership meeting/committee/sub-committee process of decision-making."
—**David Abeshouse (class of 1982)**

"Why solo? I wanted more control over my life and my cases. I'd been an assistant federal public defender, and I really liked the autonomy. But I wanted a practice environment that would let me recreate that autonomy, and where I had more freedom in the kinds of cases I did. I saw starting my own firm as an opportunity to grow a practice and learn to generate business . . . and have more control over my schedule. I've got young kids and I really like to be able to make it to their school events and their doctor's appointments. Once a week I try to pick one of them up early and have some quality, one-on-one time. I don't always make it, but I wouldn't have a shot of doing it in another setting."
—**Matthew G. Kaiser (class of 2002)**

"I wanted to be able to specialize . . . I wanted to be able to charge flat fees . . . [I wanted] the flexibility and autonomy that running my own firm brings, and as a young attorney, [I wanted] the increase in income (potential and actual)."
—**Jeffrey G. Neu (class of 2006)**

"I wanted to work for myself on the cases I chose, and I wanted to get paid completely and fully for my own efforts. Basically, I thought I could do as well or better than lawyers who were not as bright as me (and had no MBA) who were doing great on their own." —**Spencer Young (class of 2004)**

"In today's economy, everyone is expendable, and loyalty is at a pathetic minimum. If you don't perform according to someone else's standards, you are canned. I prefer to guarantee my future by creating it and being responsible for it myself.
—**Sergio Benavides (class of 2005)**

"[Why solo]? The dotcom crash had decimated Skadden Arp's telecom practice, and other firms were not interested in attorneys with my level of experience (meaning my age) unless you had a million dollars of portable business. But I was lucky. A friend at my old firm brought me in on a project that ended up being more than half of my first year's revenues."
—**Mark Del Bianco (class of 1980)**

"I practiced for 14 years, three-and-a-half at the Department of Justice and the remainder at two large law firms. I wasn't happy with my career choice after leaving DOJ. Not because there was anything wrong with my firms; they were both good places with smart, caring people, and interesting work. I just wasn't cut out for the BigLaw culture, and I wasn't comfortable in my professional skin. So, I cast about for years, trying

to figure out what else I could do. I seriously questioned whether I wanted to practice law at all, but I was unable to find anything that would interest me and pay the bills. Eventually, I decided that I had to do something else, and for the first time started seriously considering going solo. I had never seriously considered that path, but after scratching out some calculations on a pad of paper, multiplying hourly rate by billable hours, I realized that even if I didn't have a ton of work at first, the numbers were actually very favorable. So I leaped."
— **Mitchell J. Matorin (class of 1993)**

"Big law firms never appealed to me. I always wanted to start a business and work for myself. Back in law school, I clerked for big firms and small firms, but I liked the small firm lifestyle better. Once, I clerked for a solo practitioner, and she decided to spend a few weeks in Ecuador and had work sent to her via email. That really appealed to me." — **Paul Scott (class of 2008)**

"I spent over 25 years working in state government, most of them as an attorney for several different state agencies working with contractors and grantees. I had a couple of amazing bosses, but most of them were on power trips, enjoying making their staff miserable, or who were so paralyzed that they couldn't make decisions to save their souls. While I truly enjoyed my work, I became disillusioned. I had a number of offers to leave government and join different law firms, but I had no desire to get on that treadmill. I began planning to go solo about a year and a half before I left. [These days], my pension is well under half what I earned in government, and there's been no COLA in the three years since I struck out on my own. Still, having that basic income plus benefits allows me more security than

most solos. Also, as a solo, I'm guaranteed to have a tough but fair boss."
— **Jan M. Tamanini (class of 1984)**

"About a year after I left a small private practice firm, I decided to solo for several reasons: dissatisfaction with my past work environment; an inability to find a decent-paying satisfactory job (because of the poor market and a surplus of lawyers); a desire to create my own positive work environment; and a desire to 'be my own boss' . . . and eventually have a good work-life balance." — **Jenny Jeltes (class of 2006)**

"I was laid off from a good DC law firm in June 2009 after working there for six years. At first I thought about seeking employment again with a firm or with the government. I worked up a number of resumes and applied for a few positions . . . but my heart was not in it. I could barely force myself to write another cover letter stating, yet again, how I was a 'team player,' a 'self starter,' and a 'problem-solver.' I knew that I wanted to go out on my own. In a previous career, I owned several businesses in the foodservice industry, and I missed the feelings of freedom and control that goes along with being an entrepreneur. As a solo, the hours are very long right now, and my success is by no means assured. But I am enjoying the process, and I am glad I made this choice."
— **Mark Tanney (class of 1998)**

"After buying my first home only three months before, I was suddenly laid off. After a few months of no job prospects, I decided to start my bankruptcy law practice."
— **Kara O'Donnell (class of 1995)**

"Before starting a solo patent practice, I was an IP associate in BigLaw. The money was good, but after about a year I realized it was not a good fit. If I wanted a fulfilling legal practice, I would have to escape. Looking back, I think the decision had much to do with my tendency to excel when I control my own destiny, and also that I believed the future of patent preparation and prosecution was in small firms and boutiques. Going solo has exceeded my expectations in every way imaginable. I feel in control of my destiny, and my future no longer depends upon the whims of a partner. I've only been solo'ing for about a year, but I've enjoyed every single day of it. I look forward to a long, happy, AND prosperous career as a lawyer." —**Kevin Afghani (class of 2004)**

"I had no other choice (but to solo). I graduated in the middle of the pack, and, as a new lawyer at age 46, I knew no one would hire me unless I was willing to work for $30–40K, which was unacceptable for someone a family with a home, a wife, and two teenagers."
—**Dennis Esford (class of 2003)**

"Right before passing the bar I had a good, hard look at the situation—the economy, the competition for clerkships, a state hiring freeze— and I concluded that I might want to consider going out on my own. So, I asked someone I knew who [solo'd] right out of law school. He asked if I had chutzpah (well, actually, he asked me how big my balls were, so I told him very big)! He said I should be fine. So, from the time I passed the bar I started the process of going solo."
—**Lynda L. Hinkle (class of 2009)**

"Going solo right out of law school, AND practicing in a small rural town, was the last thing I wanted to do. My plan had always been to find

an associate position with a firm doing IP work. After all, what firm wouldn't want an experienced software engineer/biomedical researcher-with-multiple-graduate-degrees-turned-lawyer? As it turns out, hiring partners aren't much interested in an over-40, second career, 'night school' lawyer (actually, I took all my classes on the weekends) who graduated from a Tier 3 school. I don't think I ever had an 'Aha!' moment about solo'ing. It was more the result of the inevitable crush of circumstance and situation. Anyway, it took three months to accept the idea that if I wanted to practice it would be OK to be solo, and another five months before I gathered enough information to be comfortable with the idea, and to have the confidence to make the leap."
—**Bruce Cameron (class of 2007)**

"Some of the factors (about my going solo) were the ability to spend more time with family, the costs of commuting . . . and the fact that I have never been good with office politics."
—**Brian Rabal (class of 2005)**

"Once, briefly, I tried joining another attorney in practice. But the experience—the politics of practicing with another attorney —just reinforced my decision to be a solo. I felt that I could do better on my own, and my clientele and income immediately showed the fruition of my decision."
—**Marc W. Matheny (class of 1980)**

"For most of my career, I was a legal aid / legal services lawyer except for a brief period at a boutique firm in Manhattan. I always swore I'd never go out on my own. The thought of chasing clients for fees made me ill. I decided to open my own firm when my financial and family needs, the economy and the dearth of legal jobs, weren't a match. As a single mother, I simply could not find

2. Why did you decide to solo?

a job that paid enough to support myself AND did not have unreasonable demands. One firm would have required me to be able to stay all night on a moment's notice at the end of the day! This was not an option for a single mother whose infant had to be picked up from day care by a set time."
—**Laura S. Mann (class of 1996)**

"I decided to start a solo practice because (1) I was at a stage in life where it made sense to take a chance and start a practice (no children, unmarried, few financial obligations); (2) I was excited about the opportunity to choose the clients and cases I wanted to work on; and (3) I liked the idea of challenging myself with starting a solo practice and finding out what I could build it into."—**Tonya Coles (class of 2006)**

"I decided to solo because I was taught the importance of entrepreneurship at a very young age. I wrote a business plan for a solo practice in my second year of law school, and while I've gone off-track a few times I have generally stuck to that plan."—**Jenee Oliver (class of 2005)**

"I am not a big fan of solo practice, and frankly, I didn't decide to solo; I was forced to solo when my small, highly specialized firm was destroyed by the deregulation of the transportation industry."
—**Herb Dubin (class of 1964)**

3. What did you know about solo practice before you began?

"I knew enough to know that I didn't know much. But I also knew that thousands of lawyers all over the country were practicing as solos and they were making it work somehow."
—**Sarah Fern Meil (class of 2003)**

"I didn't know much about solo practice before I began, except that everyone I spoke to who had taken the plunge said they were much happier and would never return to a large firm."
—**Varand Gourjian (Class of 1999).**

"I had prior business experience, so I knew that if you don't bill you don't collect."
—**Bruce L. Dorner (class of 1977)**

"Everything I knew about solo'ing was based on observing colleagues who had gone on their own. I knew that every aspect of running a business would fall upon me, and I knew, too, about the risks involved. Both of which turned out to be true. But [even though] my image of solo practice was quite stereotyped, I found that no two solo practices are alike. Your practice is a reflection of your personality, and it is what you make it."
—**Kevin Afghani (class of 2004)**

"[What did I know solo'ing]? I knew that the attorneys [in solo practice] against whom I had cases seemed happier and to have higher standards of living than I did!"
—**Michael Moebes (class of 2003)**

"Before I started my solo practice, I did a lot of homework. I read every blog and piece of literature I could find on how to run and operate a law firm. By the time I actually [opened my office], I was pretty well-versed in what I needed to do to succeed."
—**Gabriel Cheong (class of 2007)**

"To the extent one can learn by reading, I knew a lot. I read Solo by Choice and other books and blogs. I spent a lot of time on the [ABA's] Solosez listserv, and I explored practice areas and office management techniques on the Internet. Basically, I tried to prepare myself. It helped, but there's no substitute for experience. My learning curve remains very steep."
—**Mark Tanney (class of 1998)**

"I planned my solo venture for two years before I opened up shop, and read everything I could find about starting and running a professional service firm, and about marketing and management. I also talked with solo practitioners about how they ran their practices." —**Dean N. (class of 1989)**

"I knew very little about solo'ing before I decided to solo myself. Shortly after making my decision, I attended a couple seminars and began networking with my colleagues." —**Jenny Jeltes (class of 2006)**

"I clerked with solo attorneys in law school, and I knew it to be a rewarding way of practicing law [even though] it required an extensive commitment to networking and managing the business side of practicing law."
—**Brian M. Annino (class of 2003)**

"I had strong organization and planning skills, and general people skills. I also knew how to ask for help from the right people."
—**Eric P. Ganci (class of 2008)**

"I had no idea how complex a solo practice would be, or that you that most of your time is spent on marketing and managing the business and a minority of time actually practicing law. Nor did I know that being a solo would be the scariest, most exhilarating, dullest, stimulating, stressful,

challenging, satisfying thing I ever attempted."
—**Bruce Cameron (class of 2007)**

"I had a few ex-colleagues in solo practice, but I didn't know them very well and they had different practice areas than mine. So, about two years before I left my government job, I got my hands on as much literature as I could from the bar and the Internet. And I read a lot about marketing for small businesses, and about having a private consulting business. Even though those aren't traditional areas for attorneys to master, my sense was that to be even moderately successful at a solo transactional practice, I would have to understand the essentials of these business areas."
—**Jan M. Tamanini (class of 1984)**

"Before I made the decision to solo, I spoke to a lot of other solo attorneys, and I read a lot of material on various aspects of a solo career. I knew that the isolation was going to be tough; I knew that I was going to have to be extremely aggressive marketing my business, and had to be prepared to take advantage of whatever opportunities popped up (even on the weekend); and I knew that certain tasks might take me longer to accomplish without the resources and supervision that comes with a multi-lawyer firm. Most importantly, my research helped me to understand that building a solo practice would take time, dedication and a lot of work."
—**Adam Neufer (class of 2009)**

"Solo practice wasn't presented as a career option in law school. It seems ridiculous to me now, but it was just assumed we would all go into law firms and serve a partner for 8-10 years before even taking our own cases. I knew next to nothing [about solo'ing]. So, I started to follow such resources as the ABA's Solosez listserv,

3. What did you know about solo practice before you began?

Carolyn Elefant's blog (MyShingle.com) and BuildASoloPractice.com, and I found the support that I needed from these pioneers."
—**Stephanie Kimbro (class of 2003)**

"Prior to getting laid off I hedged my bets! I got admitted to the Federal Court, and began taking some bankruptcy cases through the pro bono program with which I was affiliated. Since they provided training and access to bankruptcy mentors, it was a win-win for me. As for the day-to-day activities of solo lawyering, I knew nothing! However, I had known many an entrepreneur, and I knew that starting any business would take creativity, belief in self . . . and lots of hard work."
—**Kara O'Donnell (class of 1995)**

"I worked for a small firm for 2 1/2 years during law school. During that time I got a good idea of how a solo attorney allocates his time."
—**Lael Brown (class of 2009)**

"I had some idea what was involved because I ran a business before. Other than that, I read a couple of books [about solo'ing], but that was it!"
—**Lynda L. Hinkle (class of 2009)**

4. How did you explain your decision to colleagues?

"Most of my former government colleagues (particularly the other attorneys) thought I was crazy and wondered, 'What the hell are you thinking?' They couldn't understand why I wanted to leave a job with good pay and great benefits. They thought I was blowing smoke and wouldn't follow through. But [after 25+ years], I just couldn't stay in a safe but soul-sucking environment. Don't get me wrong; if you work for a large company, agency, or firm that values its employees, there may be no better place in the world to work. But staying in a place that makes you hate coming to work every day just to get a regular paycheck can make you crazy." —**Jan M. Tamanini (class of 1984)**

"[I told colleagues] that I didn't want to regret not giving [solo practice] a try, and that my mid-30's was the best time to take a risk. 'It's not you; it's me!' I said. I gave two months notice instead of two weeks, and I tried to settle or try as many cases as I could before I left."
—**Michael Moebes (class of 2003)**

"I didn't explain myself to anyone except my husband, and I told him that I didn't want to hear any negative talk about [opening a solo practice]. I was just going to do it, and if it didn't work we would worry about it then."
—**Lynda L. Hinkle (class of 2009)**

"Many [of my colleagues] were surprised. Give up the weekly paycheck and the health insurance? How dare I rock the boat! But the time was right to start my firm, so I chose to take the risk rather than to look for another uninspired job with a paycheck and a few benefits."
—**Kara O'Donnell (class of 1995)**

"I just said that [going solo] is what I always wanted to do; that I was following a dream.

I got many different types of reactions; mostly positive. Most people were envious. They told me that they wish they could have done it, or that they would like to; some said they just don't have the guts to [solo]." **—Paul Scott (class of 2008)**

"I explained that I needed to have a flexible work schedule so that I could spend more time with my kids. Many thought I was nuts, and I'm sure a few of them thought I just didn't have any other options. The truth is I only applied to three or four positions before deciding I wanted to solo. Now, the practice of law is ever so much more meaningful [because] I get to interact and help my clients directly without worrying about meeting my billing quota." **—Lael Brown (class of 2009)**

"A lot of my colleagues [classmates] were in the same situation as me: too inexperienced to secure an associate position, and too experienced to be hired as a paralegal, clerk or administrative employee. Really, the only option left (besides surfing the want-ads all day) was to create my own job. The simple reality of the lousy state of the economy obviated any need to explain myself. In fact, I did more encouraging than explaining. I tried to get more of my classmates to go solo, or at least persuade them into believing they were capable of it." **—Adam Neufer (class of 2009)**

"When I was growing up, I lived in a small town in Iowa. Many of my parents' friends were lawyers. I loved their attitude toward their clients and their life. They just seemed independent and free in a way that lawyers in other practice settings don't often seem to be. [When the time came], I told people that I wanted to create an environment where I could do that and be that."
—Matthew G. Kaiser (class of 2002)

Should you reveal your plans at work?

Unless one of your colleagues at work is a personal friend, it's best NOT to reveal your plans prior to leaving (the obvious exception being if you discover that another colleague wants to solo, and you decide to partner up).

Once a firm hears of a possible departure, the partners assume the worst and usually activate all their defense systems to secure clients, supplies, and other firm resources. Why would a firm be afraid of your going solo? Because law firms are one giant living ego, and any threat—no matter how remote—usually raises suspicion. If you're more senior, with a couple of clients, your firm has even more reason to tighten ranks. So, be discrete about revealing your plans at work.

The other reason to be less than candid about your plans is the naysaying from colleagues. Just at a time when your deliberations are fresh and your optimism high, your colleagues may try to convince you that your plans are nothing less than career suicide. Or, if you work for a government agency or claims department, where risk-averse colleagues are biding their time in dead-end jobs, they might be quick to point out the folly of leaving the security of a solid job. You might even encounter naysaying from solos themselves. Disgruntled or unsuccessful solos may try to discourage you from starting a firm because they can't stand the idea that you might succeed where they could not.

"My former colleagues have been supportive. I think some of them hear the call of the solo themselves, but they're not yet ready to make the move. Still, they would like to see me succeed partly so that they can believe that the solo path is possible." —**Mark Tanney (class of 1998)**

"The one person outside of my family who has been both an encouraging and inspiring force was another patent attorney who had already established his own solo practice, and who provided me with contract patent work while I built my practice. He is a huge advocate for doing things outside of the accepted mold, and I was encouraged by the fact that someone with this philosophy had been so successful."
—**Kevin Afghani (class of 2004)**

"A very dear friend has seen me through college, marriage, law school, an MBA, a cushy six-figure job that made me miserable, and a less lucrative 'real firm' job that made me equally miserable. When I finally decided to hang my shingle, she was one of my biggest supporters because she knew me well enough to know having my own shop would make me happy. Even when I was making six-figures for embarrassingly little responsibility, I was simply unhappy. She was and is still one of my best cheerleaders."
—**Gina Bongiovi (class of 2007)**

"My wife. Without her support, [my solo practice] never would have worked." —**Bruce L. Dorner** (class of 1977)

"My law school mentor. He's gone out of his way to be supportive and encouraging. On everything from helping me find office space to being there for countless 'how-do-I do-this' and 'I'm-really-in-a-panic' sessions. He's even thrown work my way when my practice starts to lag. One of these days, I'll figure out how to thank him."
—**Bruce Cameron (class of 2007)**

"Outside of my family, my professors—and especially my law school's career service center—have offered tremendous support and encouragement. My former classmates were also a great source of support (and referrals)."
—**Adam Neufer (class of 2009)**

"[In my experience] the most supportive people have been the amazing people in the community of solo and small firm attorneys whom I've met through bar activities; in particular those participating in the Pennsylvania Bar Association's Solo Small Firm Practice Section listserv and the ABA's Solosez listserv. The online solo/small firm community is immensely supportive and serves as a lifeline on many issues, especially involving practice management."
—**Jan M. Tamanini (class of 1984)**

"[For me, the most supportive] was an attorney I met through a local solo/small firm group that held monthly dinners, which I had stumbled upon by hanging around a couple of email listservs. (A big shout-out to Andrea Goldman!) There is also a very supportive network of local solo attorneys, and an entire national family of supportive solos through the Solosez listserv."
—**Mitchell J. Matorin (class of 1993)**

"Outside of my family, my colleagues have been the most supportive because they understand how scary it is to be completely on your own! I steer clear of people who do not support it. [In fact], I could never date someone who is not supportive of this endeavor."
—**Jenny Jeltes (class of 2006)**

5. Who was the most supportive of your decision?

"The person I share an office with. We have back-to-back office chairs (it's a small office), so she likes to say she has my back inside and outside the office! I'm very grateful for her."
—**Lynda L. Hinkle (class of 2009)**

"One lawyer friend who solo'd before me was supportive. But not many [others]. [Some] lawyers thought I was a little nuts."
—**Thomas J. Crane (class of 1983)**

"My immediate family actually was not that supportive in my decision to start my own practice. My mother thought that I was too young and too inexperienced, and that no one would hire me. It wasn't until my second year of practice that she could see that what I was building could succeed." —**Gabriel Cheong (class of 2007)**

6. What are your sharpest memories of starting out?

"I remember thinking,'Why didn't I do this five years earlier?'"—**Walter D. James III (class of 1987)**

"I remember depositing a retainer check the first day I was open, and marveling that I'd already covered my expenses for the month."
—**Matthew G. Kaiser (class of 2002)**

"[I remember the] fear. And the periodic and overwhelming sense that I had taken on more than I could handle. But . . . I also absolutely loved it right from the start, and I knew that if I could stick with it through the learning curve, I would be very happy on my own."
—**Cailie A. Currin (class of 1988)**

"I remember worrying that my contract assignments would suddenly end with no replacement in sight. But a week after my first assignment, I had another . . . and I have been working continuously ever since."
—**Denny Esford (class of 2003)**

"I remember having a lot of free time and smoking a lot of cigars." —**Varand Gourjian (class of 1999)**

"My first month was a blur. That first year was definitely a struggle: setting up the technology, the business accounts, working out Web sites and letterheads. I didn't have time to look around. By the end of my first year, it was evident that I had done a lot to lay the foundation, but now I had to really build a successful firm on top of it."
—**Gabriel Cheong (class of 2007)**

"The first month was a blur. So much to do, and not enough hours in the day to do it. I remember having my first meeting with a potential client and not knowing when I would even have time to do legal work. Luckily I got everything set up and scheduled my days in such a way that I would block out portions of the day to do legal work, marketing, etc." —**Paul Scott (class of 2008)**

"That first month or so was very challenging. I remember feeling scared and self-conscious. Luckily, I kept my expenses low and tried to take as many fixed-fee and retainer cases as possible. I also started practicing in New Orleans post-Katrina, and this was actually very fortunate. During that period, many attorneys there were still displaced, and there was a lot of business coming into the city to help with the rebuilding. I took a few insurance dispute cases on contingency, and used that client base to find other clients who needed LLCs, contracts, and the like. I also had two quick settlements that put some breath into my firm's lungs, and from there I consciously grew my non-contingency work load as I grew the contingency end." —**Scott Wolfe (class of 2005)**

"[Those first few months of solo'ing] I ate dinner at a lot of those all-you-can-eat, happy hour-complimentary buffets."
—**Marc W. Matheny (class of 1980)**

"It was a rough time. For the first eight months, I waited with almost unbearable anticipation for the phone to ring. When it did, I felt like hiding under my desk. I was stuck between the excitement of building my business and the terror that I would screw something up. For a few months —especially in the beginning —the fear was almost paralyzing. I'd find myself in tears some days, wondering what I'd done; whether I'd made the right decision to start my own firm, or to even attend law school." —**Gina Bongiovi (class of 2007)**

"There was an intense rawness to those first days and months [of solo practice]. It was a time of

second-guessing, and feeling at sea with the fear of calamity mere moments away (actually, it was a bit like Civil Procedure). I do have fond memories, though, of those clients who allowed me to learn and earn on their dime. But my sharpest memories are more internal than external: the feeling of dread when I walked into the office each morning; the elation of that first client; the surprise when I got a referral; the exhilaration that came from getting a positive result for a client; and the contentment of earning that first fee. I also remember learning that being an advocate didn't mean I had to always find a legal solution for client when common sense advice was all that was needed." —**Bruce Cameron (class of 2007)**

"I was so proud. I wore my 3-piece suit to work every day . . . even if I had no clients. Now (after 30+ years in practice), an open-collar shirt is the norm!" —**Bruce L. Dorner (class of 1977)**

"[What do I remember]? I made some costly mistakes that first year thinking I had to advertise like a traditional law firm. I took out a Yellow Pages ad and subscribed to a popular online directory for my new firm. I dropped $4,000, and maybe received one referral. [I also remember] feeling insecure before sending the client that final work product. I was so used to having another associate or paralegal at the firm glance at documents before they went out to the client, but when you're a solo it's only your own set of eyes. It took many months to build up the confidence without agonizing over every little detail." —**Stephanie Kimbro (class of 2003)**

"[I remember] a mad scramble to learn everything there was to learn and making it all happen. What a whirlwind! But it was lots of fun."
—**Laura S. Mann (class of 1996)**

"[I remember] the panic of not knowing how I would develop clientele, and the uncertainty of figuring out how to comply with all the various laws and regulations associated with being a lawyer." —**Jeffrey G. Neu (class of 2006)**

"[I remember] the ups and downs: having many new prospects call in a single day, and then have no one call for a week or two. I also remember working late nights to file bankruptcy cases, and then realizing happily that I could sleep late the next morning. After all I was a solo! [What I failed to consider] is that bankruptcy court usually calls at 8:30 a.m. Now, I work into the wee hours only if I can answer calls in a coherent fashion at 8:00 the next morning."
—**Kara O'Donnell (class of 1995)**

"[I remember] appearing in court for my first trial. I was super-nervous, but I realized I can do this! Now, 20 years later on my second go-around as a solo, my sharpest memory is appearing back in what we call Presiding Court, where we hold motions, and seeing many of the same familiar faces; a little older but very familiar. It's comforting being back where I feel I belong." —**Thomas J. Crane (class of 1983)**

"[I remember] the excitement. That I was having the experience I worked so hard for while in law school."—**Brian M. Annino (class of 2003)**

"I remember feeling very overwhelmed. [Especially with] all the things I needed to do to get my practice started. [On top of that], I had just given up a BigLaw salary which I was growing quite accustomed to. I've spoken to [other] solos who said they experienced panic about whether they would make it financially. These moments are natural, and can sometimes be a strong motivating force in building your practice."
—**Kevin Afghani (class of 2004)**

"Those first days were exciting, exhilarating. But I was also stressed about not having my office set up 'just so'. [I also remember] being grateful for the first few referrals I got, and for the lawyers who were willing to have lunch with me and dole out advice." —**Michael Moebes (class of 2003)**

"[Those first few months] were exciting and terrifying. Exciting to set up the office, choose furniture, get stationery and business cards, make contacts, network; terrifying [when I] wondered if I would be able to make ends meet and have enough clients to sustain a practice."
—**Abbe W. McClane (class of 2003)**

"I experienced a lot of frustration those first few months. Tons of bad intake consultations, and I had to deal with free-loaders who wanted free legal advice. I also recall having clients agree to representation only to back out at the last minute." —**Sergio Benavides (class of 2005)**

"When I first went solo, representing clients without supervision was an anxiety-producer. Although I had a good amount of experience in my chosen field, calling the shots and making the hard decisions required an extreme amount of confidence that I did not have after I passed the Bar and decided to go solo. My first case was a multi-day trial for which I had only two weeks to prepare. Now that someone was actually depending on me to represent them, [I had] no time to get muddled down in fear and self-doubt. While it is important to recognize your weaknesses and areas where you might need to call in some help, self-doubt is extremely dangerous for solo practitioners, and can get them in a ton of trouble! The trial taught me to trust my instincts. Without trial experience or any real experience as an actual attorney, my instincts

6. What are your sharpest memories of starting out?

were all I had—and those instincts helped me win the trial. —**Adam Neufer (class of 2009)**

"I had planned to use the first several months after leaving my government job for planning and getting my house in order, both figuratively and literally. But an acquaintance asked me for assistance with a commercial dispute where both parties had allowed a small problem to grow into a monster, and that was not a good way to start my solo practice. I should have stuck to my guns and refused the work while following through with my original plan to get the practice set up as I wanted it to be before taking clients." —**Jan M. Tamanini (class of 1984)**

"When I sat in my office that first week, I remember the mixed feelings I had (excitement, anxiety, etc.). I was worried about my ability to bring in clients and meet expenses. But I also felt an overwhelming sense of freedom; freedom to do what I wanted with my practice. It was a great feeling that I often feel today." —**Tonya Coles (class of 2006)**

"I'm still in my first few months of practice, so my sharpest memories are not too far removed. I think that I will always remember the feeling of doing everything for the first time: creating law firm forms and other client materials; setting up a Web site and blog; purchasing supplies and equipment; registering my business with the city; opening bank accounts; joining organizations; attending meetings, seminars and CLE's; marketing; and continuing my study of the substantive law. Everything is new, everything is urgent. Each day I feel like I am completing only half of my 'must-do' list for the day." —**Mark Tanney (class of 1998)**

"My first year as a solo was the worst financial experience of my career."
—**Herb Dubin (class of 1964)**

7. What sacrifices did you make to solo?

"I sacrificed my personal life for a good couple of years."—**Jeffrey G. Neu (class of 2006)**

"I gave up a BigLaw salary and a regular paycheck for no guaranteed income at no guaranteed time. [The sacrifice] was worth every penny."
—**Kevin Afghani (class of 2004)**

"I gave up a six-figure income and some of my benefits, and I left a bustling workplace and the downtown social scene. Sometimes the isolation gets to me. But most of the time I'm just happy to not have to deal with the time-suckers, the back-stabbers, the political sycophants, and all the others who made my government career less than enjoyable in the last few years."
—**Jan M. Tamanini (class of 1984)**

"Money is the first and most significant sacrifice. Two years in and I'm still not making the money I want. However, I chose to laser-focus my practice area, and I don't dabble in other areas. This way, I have sacrificed a lot in potential revenue, but I have also become the go-to person for my practice area. And even though clients don't come along as often, the clients I do get now are higher quality."
—**Gina Bongiovi (class of 2007)**

"I was so happy to be on my own that the pay cut, and the uncertainty [of solo'ing], didn't seem like a sacrifice to me. The biggest sacrifice was made by my family, giving up the (perception of) security that comes with a law firm salary, the pension plan, and everything else that goes with that career path."—**Cailie A. Currin (class of 1988)**

"[Sacrifice]? I didn't take vacations the first year. I missed several concerts, and birthday presents for the kids were often used or nonexistent."
—**Michael Moebes (class of 2003)**

"I can't go to restaurants like I used to, and my hair stylist forgot my name. But business is improving . . . slowly. It takes a while to develop that happy client base that will refer you to new clients. It's been nine months and I just got my first one of those yesterday."
—**Kara O'Donnell (class of 1995)**

"[What did I sacrifice]? Job and financial security . . . although in this economy that seems to be absent in the lives of most people."
—**Adam Neufer (class of 2009)**

"Financially, we downsized and reined in our standard of living considerably. We sold our house and moved to a rented townhouse half the size. I mostly work seven days a week right now (and lose a fair amount of sleep)."
—**Mark Tanney (class of 1998)**

"I sacrificed time for myself. I've cancelled several vacations and days off because 'something comes up' at the office. It's temporary, though, because at some point I will have staff to assist."
—**Tonya Coles (class of 2006)**

"My biggest sacrifice is that I spend too much time at the office and too little time with my family. This is the nature of the beast, and any solo who says he or she doesn't spend more time in practice than a 35-40 hour work week is lying."
—**Marc W. Matheny (class of 1980)**

"The biggest 'sacrifice' has been of perceived prestige. Like most law students, I was indoctrinated that success is measured by the name of your firm and the size of your paycheck. It took some time to get my mind around the idea that it might not be so, and the number of big firm attorneys who have told me that they envy me, or

who have sought me out to talk about my career path, never ceases to amaze me."
—**Mitchell J. Matorin (class of 1993)**

"I work early in the morning or late at night to maintain the work/life balance I want. Right now the sacrifice is sleep . . . but that may have more to do with trying to run a solo practice and having young children. For the first three years our family sacrificed by not spending like we would have if I had a kept a steady law firm job. It was not easy, but we stayed in a house that was too small for our growing family, and didn't upgrade things like TV, car, or clothes. Now almost five years later, we are in a better place and glad we made those sacrifices as a family." —**Stephanie Kimbro (class of 2003)**

"I expected to be living on a shoestring budget for the first year. But the other sacrifice I made was unexpected: it was the amount of time required to be a solo. Working on Saturdays all day pretty much goes without saying, and for me working for most of Sunday is pretty much a norm as well. Obviously, I don't want to work seven days a week 24 hours a day my entire life, but I am willing to do it while I build the practice."
—**Paul Scott (class of 2008)**

"It's not a 'sacrifice' as much as making trade-offs or substitutions. For example, date night for my wife and I changed from restaurants and theater tickets to take-out and a rented DVD. And those leisurely two week vacations are now a hectic three-day weekend. [I have no doubt] that what I am postponing during these early stages [as a solo] will return as my life progresses. I'm walking a new path, and I accept that this new path requires changes, putting aside old pursuits, reevaluating my priorities, and refocusing and rethinking my desires." —**Bruce Cameron (class of 2007)**

" . . . Flat-fee investigations."
—**Sergio Benavides (class of 2005)**

" . . . Contract lawyering."
—**Spencer Young (class of 2004)**

" . . . Document reviews for large-scale litigation."
—**Dennis Esford (class of 2003)**

"... I dipped into my savings."
—**Nina Kallen (class of 1994)**

"Clients who came with me from my former firm, and I also jumped head-first into business and legal networking which helped me grow my practice." —**David Abeshouse (class of 1982)**

"With the help of personal savings, some estate-planning work, and a few appearances for a local solo attorney, I was able to pay my rent from the start."
—**Sarah Fern Meil (class of 2003)**

"I wouldn't say I had a revenue stream, it was more like a revenue drip."
—**Traci D. Ellis (class of 1990)**

"I started off with a few clients. It was enough to pay the bills, which totaled under $1,000 a month. After the first month, I was able to start paying myself a salary. [Now] I spend half my time marketing/networking to keep bringing clients in."
—**Lynda L. Hinkle (class of 2009)**

"I did contract patent work for other law firms. Getting [the work] was actually quite easy, but it also kept me from doing the business development I needed to get my own practice off the ground." —**Kevin Afghani (class of 2004)**

"I kept working at my old job, going from full-time to part-time. With a second job, I was able to build my practice without worrying about health insurance and retirement benefits. There's a downside to a second job, though: managing two schedules requires judicious use of vacation days, frank communication [with clients], and a great deal of flexibility. A second job also reduced the number of hours I was able to spend developing, marketing, and working at my practice, so my practice grows at a slower rate."
—**Bruce Cameron (class of 2007)**

"I had some savings, I was getting unemployment for a short time, and I got a moderate SBA Line of Credit to tide me over. Then the clients, and the fees, starting coming."
—**Laura S. Mann (class of 1996)**

"I did contract work for a local non-profit. It was my only guaranteed income. It didn't pay much, but I enjoyed the work, and it has lead to a lot of referral sources. I am a big believer in the idea that 'work generates work which generates work'. By taking a small pro bono case from the non-profit agency, [it may] lead to an extremely happy client who is going to refer two or three people to you (who are paying clients)."
—**Paul Scott (class of 2008)**

"A couple really busy attorneys in my field paid me hourly to handle oral arguments, hearings, and mediations when they had to be somewhere else. I also became a financial counselor and did 'money coaching' for extra income."
—**Michael Moebes (class of 2003)**

"The first time around [as a solo], I relied on court appointments. We do not have a public defender program in San Antonio. So, judges would appoint lawyers to represent criminal defendants. I did that just about everyday, and it was a great way to get into court and get over that huge fear. And I did cases representing children taken by the state or their parents. My second time around as a solo, I now rely on my blog, on letters to other lawyers, and on a couple of good referral services."

—**Thomas J. Crane (class of 1983)**

"[In the beginning of my solo practice], I talked with as many people as possible about what I was doing. Every social occasion, every networking event, every possible opportunity, was a chance to mention my business. I honed my 'elevator speech' so that when someone asked what I did for a living, I had a coherent, interesting answer. I asked friends for business; I asked for referrals. And I distinguished my practice from what other attorneys in the area were doing. [My advice]: keep reminding people about your value and services, and many will eventually come around. But one contact is not enough; it usually takes several 'touches' to get someone interested."

—**Jan M. Tamanini (class of 1984)**

Can you afford to solo?

From a financial perspective, the thought of starting a firm can seem daunting. Not only must you replace the lost income stream, but you carry the burden of everything from computer equipment and office supplies to malpractice insurance, health insurance, and retirement contributions. What follows are some preliminary considerations:

What are your business prospects?

Even as you start thinking about starting your own firm, it's important to analyze any immediate business prospects you may have. Of course, you can't solicit firm clients when you're still working at the firm, but you do need to look critically at which, if any, clients, are likely to follow you to a new practice, or maybe you know other attorneys who might refer cases to you or send you contract work. But don't worry if you don't have a single client on the horizon because you really don't need many billable hours to get started. Let's say that starting out you can find only one day's worth of billable work a week or one flat-fee matter (like a bankruptcy case or estate plan) every two weeks. At $150/hour, that's $1,200/week or around $1,500 to $2,500 every two weeks (or more, depending on the billable rate in your area). That's gross revenue; you've still got taxes and overhead. But still, if you trim your costs, you should be able to capture some profit from Day 1.

Should you start a practice part-time?

To make ends meet, many new solos consider working part-time at a law-related job while their practice is getting off the ground. Others, by necessity, find part-time work. Some argue that a solo law practice requires full-time commitment for success, and that working at it part-time compromises that commitment. Whether it's true or not in your own case, the revenue from part-time work will provide some financial security as you get your practice off the ground. And with that (along with some other revenue stream), you may feel less pressured to take any case that walks in the door, or to recommend a less-than-ideal settlement just so you can get paid.

8. How did you create a revenue stream in the beginning?

8. How did you create a revenue stream in the beginning?

"My practice was, and still is, heavily dependent on referrals from other solo attorneys, and from my old firm (a word of advice: never burn bridges). With a litigation practice, it only takes one or two cases to get a reasonably consistent and lasting revenue stream. If I had a transactional practice or a family-oriented practice where I had to hustle for each client and each client offered only a discrete revenue potential, things would have been far more difficult for me."
—**Mitchell J. Matorin (class of 1993)**

"Unemployment was paying me while I was deciding to move forward with my plan [to solo]."
—**Kara O'Donnell (class of 1995)**

"For the first three months I've only had three clients. Luckily, each had matters involving litigation, which can be a lot of hours and a lot of work. Because I've been so busy I haven't had time to advertise, so I need to start looking into that . . . now." —**Lael Brown (class of 2009)**

"Since I have been working from home, and my husband is the primary breadwinner, I haven't felt the pressure to bring in a certain amount each month, which has been great since things took off slowly. I have several regular legal writing clients (for whom I write blogs), which provide a nice income stream." —**Sarah White (class of 2002)**

"In the beginning, before I had a lot of divorce and estate planning cases, my main source of income was real estate closings. I don't like doing real estate closings but it was quick money. In the month leading up to my grand opening, I contacted over a hundred lenders, title and loan companies, and signed up with them to do out of state real estate closings for them when I started my practice. It took a lot of time to get contacts with all of those companies, but once I did the legwork I had my bread and butter for the first year." —**Herb Dubin (class of 1964)**

"I kept my marketing company alive while I got the law firm off the ground. I used the revenue from the marketing company to fund startup expenses for the law firm." —**Gina Bongiovi (class of 2007)**

"As a new solo, it was more important to me to get a client to sign the retainer agreement than to make a large profit. There is a lot of competition out there, and I was too afraid of scaring a potential client off with a large fee. So, I made an effort to get a sense of the individual's financial circumstances, and tailored my fee to what I thought he or she could afford. I offered discounted rates and flat-rate fees. But I was always stern once I set a fee and never negotiated with the client. I also knew it was important to get as much money up front so I required deposits. This practice helped me avoid having to chase clients for money. When there was a shortage of business, I did contract work for other firms."
—**Adam Neufer (class of 2009)**

"I started by telling family members, friends, and former colleagues that I started a practice. I sent letters containing contact information and an explanation of my practice areas. In the beginning, my sole source of referrals was family and friends." —**Tonya Coles (class of 2006)**

"In the beginning, I brought in most of my revenue from Court appointments and close family and friends." —**Jenee Oliver (class of 2005)**

"It took nine months to a year for me to make a profit. Even though I made expensive marketing mistakes, I finally found one print magazine that met my target client base and I stuck with that. It pulled in a steady two-to-three clients a month. [Thereafter], I started using online forums, listservs and blogs as a way to connect with other attorneys in my state that might lead to referrals. I made up a chart of weekly and then monthly online 'tasks' for marketing my practice. I stayed consistent with them and after a while it started to pay off." —**Stephanie Kimbro (class of 2003)**

"I just got started, so I'm not anywhere close to having a 'stream' of revenue. My goal is to eventually have my practice become profitable enough so I no longer need to do boring contract document review work!"
—**Jenny Jeltes (class of 2006)**

"I was very lucky. I was able to work out an 'of counsel' arrangement with my former firm, and I had one corporate client that gave me a significant retainer fee payment. I felt pretty confident that I would have at least some money coming in."
—**Cailie A. Currin (class of 1988)**

PART TWO:
A Day in the Life

9. What role does a spouse/partner play in a solo's success?

10. How do you balance parenting with a solo practice?

11. What practice skills were you least prepared for?

12. What was your most difficult client experience, and what did you learn?

13. Should new lawyers open a solo practice?

14. What was your biggest goof, and what did it teach you?

15. What important issues do new solos face?

16. What role does risk play in a solo practice?

17. What are the biggest challenges when you're the boss?

18. What do you like/dislike about the autonomy of solo practice?

19. What frustrations are solos likely to experience?

20. What role do mentors play in your practice?

21. What role do people skills play in a solo's success?

Introduction

When you accept an offer at a law firm, in-house or government agency, you have a pretty good idea what to expect. You know roughly how many hours you're expected to work, how much you will earn, where you will be working, and who you will be working with.

By contrast, the day-in-day-out details of practicing solo remain a mystery for so many lawyers thinking about starting their own firm. Either because they don't know any other solos, or because those they do know haven't been entirely candid in sharing the downside of their practice; the kooky clients, the embarrassing moments, the stupid mistakes. In that regard, this section is especially valuable because it draws back the curtains on the solo experience . . . not just at the office, but on the home front as well.

9. What role does a spouse/partner play in a solo's success?

"My wife has been and still is an amazing pillar of support for me. More than anyone, she encouraged me to go out on my own . . . and kept encouraging me when I got cold feet. She also is a part-time legal assistant, helping me around the office when I fall behind or just need help."
—**Paul Scott (class of 2008)**

"My wife gave me the final nudge of courage I needed to quit my job and go solo. Before that conversation in the kitchen in January 2009, my going solo was always followed by 'someday.'"
—**Michael Moebes (class of 2003)**

"My wife plays a huge role. I could not have gone solo without her because she covers our costs of living. Her paychecks take care of food and mortgage, which made launching my practice possible. She also has to tolerate the huge risk that my practice poses, from liability for malpractice to waiting a long time to resolve contingency fee cases. Without her support, I simply could not be doing what I do."
—**Brian T. Pedigo (class of 2007)**

"If it weren't for my wife's support, I don't think I would have made it through law school . . . much less have the courage to go solo. She allows me to keep juggling all the balls simply because I know that she's there to catch one from time to time. So, how do would I characterize her role? The best I can do is say that besides providing moral and emotional support, she is my unpaid office manager/chief assistant/proofreader/receptionist/billing department/all around 'gal Friday.'" —**Bruce Cameron (class of 2007)**

"My fiancé was critical in my decision to go solo. To this day I do not think I would've done it without her support. Since she herself is a patent

attorney, she understood very well the stresses that come with being in a law firm. She saw the perfect fit between me and solo practice even before I myself had realized it. As I was to find out, breaking out on my own comes with a huge set of risks where nothing is guaranteed and everything is in flux. With this kind of wild uncertainty as to the future, a supportive partner is sometimes the sole stabilizing force that keeps you sane. My fiancé helped me to make this important decision, and she makes sure that I stick it through and always performing my A game."
— **Kevin Afghani (class of 2004)**

"If it wasn't for my husband's support, I wouldn't have been able to go on my own. The financial hit we took while I got the firm started wasn't easy, and the emotional turmoil I put myself through wasn't easy either. Watching me vacillate between elation and terror was pretty rough on him because he couldn't really do anything to help. Now that I've come through that fog, for the most part, he reminds me now and then of the fear I felt and how I got through it."
— **Gina Bongiovi (class of 2007)**

"My husband is a huge part of the dance that my family does every day. He has to be flexible with me or it won't work. When I have a deadline or need to get something to a client quickly, he rearranges his schedule and picks up the kids or drives them to their activities, and gives me that extra time." — **Stephanie Kimbro (class of 2003)**

"My biggest concern is always, 'What work will I have after I finish this?' I can estimate what I'll make next month based on my current workload, but six months from now I have no idea. It's very risky. I am lucky because my husband brings home a regular paycheck, making it possible for me to

do this. I don't know if I would be willing to do it this way without him."
— **Lael Brown (class of 2009)**

"My husband plays a huge role. My daughters are still young, and he is the primary breadwinner. He also helps with child care when I meet a client or need to get work done. I literally could not do it without him." — **Sarah White (class of 2002)**

"If you've got kids, I don't know how you could solo without a seriously supportive spouse. It's a lot of time away from the family, and sometimes, even when you're with the family, you're away from the family. I just couldn't do it without a supportive partner."
— **Matthew G. Kaiser (class of 2002)**

"[The role of a spouse/partner]? A very important role, especially since we were both practicing law at different firms, and our son was seven years old. We developed a routine of synchronizing our schedules once a week to make sure that one or the other of us was always available to pick up our son from school and to take him to his own events. About a year after I started my office, I hired my wife." — **Dean N. Alterman (class of 1989)**

"Without support at home, it would be very difficult to be a solo. My spouse has had to put up with late nights and occasional weekend work as well as very occasionally missing a child's ballgame or recital. It is not easy on my spouse, and I know it." — **Marc W. Matheny (class of 1980)**

"Spouses are KEY to having a solo practice. My first husband was not supportive at all, and did not pick up any household chores, so I was pretty much in charge of everything. It was a terrible drain and hindered my ability to grow my

practice. My second husband has been terribly supportive —in terms of helping me think like a businessperson, in terms of marketing, helping the technology side of my practice, and helping make sure the household chores are done. I have so much more energy to devote to my practice with a supportive husband!"
—**D. Jill Pugh (class of 1994)**

"Starting a solo practice is such an all-consuming process that the spouse plays a big role —either positive or negative —regardless of whether he or she wants to. A supportive spouse will help you through the hard times and possibly provide a financial bridge during start up. A skeptical or reluctant spouse can be a drain on your energy and emotional resources. Your spouse's views should be carefully considered before you head down this road." —**Mark Tanney (class of 1998)**

"My partner plays a vital role in my solo practice. It is because of my partner, in large part, that going solo was even possible. Setting up a solo practice requires a good amount of start-up capital. If your practice does not generate income immediately, and you do not have a nest egg, it is extremely difficult to make anything happen. I was fortunate that my partner was able to relieve some of the financial burden of starting a solo practice. Spouses and partners can play other important roles. For me, one of the most difficult aspects of being a solo practitioner is the isolation. I do not have other attorneys or staff members to share the responsibilities of managing my firm, so I rely on my partner to discuss marketing ideas and other matters of my business. It's also great to have your own personal cheerleader."
—**Adam Neufer (class of 2009)**

"Spouses play a HUGE ROLE. A spouse / partner must understand missed meals, missed social events, reduced income, bad cash flow, and no 'free' benefits. In my case, after fully raising two children (in college), and having a third child in elementary school, my wife found a job in the Federal government outside her training and experience, just so that we could get health insurance for a family of five."
—**Herb Dubin (class of 1964)**

"Soloing gives me the flexibility to spend a lot of time with my daughters. At the same time, I wonder constantly if I'm spending enough time on my practice. It's a balancing act, as I'm sure it is with any job. But soloing gives me the flexibility I wouldn't have with a regular law firm job."
—**Sarah White (class of 2002)**

"Balance? I've got twins! You just do the best you can, and you don't take in cases that you can't handle well, efficiently, and competently."
—**Bruce L. Dorner (class of 1977)**

"As a single mother, I found starting and having my own practice to be very tough, very challenging . . . and very scary. The fear of not knowing when or if a paying client will walk through the doors can be overwhelming at times, especially when I am the sole source of income. On the other hand, it also has been very exciting and most gratifying as well. My daughter's day care is in my office building and this Friday, for example, I am chaperoning their school field trip."
—**Laura S. Mann (class of 1996)**

"[One of the reasons I decided to solo] was to have the flexibility to have dinner with the family most every night, and pull out the MacBook after the children went to bed. When I was at a defense firm, I missed a lot of dinners and bedtimes."
—**Michael Moebes (class of 2003)**

"[As a single parent], it's more than a little unnerving not having a guaranteed monthly income when you have kids who insist on eating every day, [and on top of that] a mortgage and living expenses. [As a solo], it's great to be able to control my own schedule—somewhat—and to be able to guarantee that I can attend certain things. On the other hand, I also feel compelled to work

late because everything depends on me, with the unfortunate result that I'm usually not home for dinner. Somewhere there's a happy medium . . . but I haven't found it yet."
—**Mitchell J. Matorin (class of 1993)**

"I am much more able to meet the demands of parenting a teenager in my own practice than in a firm . . . but it is still hard. [And while] I love the freedom to decide my priorities on any given day, I still have to make trade-offs. But at least I know that I'm the one making them and taking responsibility for them. For me, the biggest challenge is the travel that comes along with actively marketing my practice. I'm on the road for a few days every month, and that takes its toll on the family. But that has been my trade-off and the choice that I made."
—**Cailie A. Currin (class of 1988)**

"It is sometimes difficult as a solo who works from home to shut down the work side of the brain. Sometimes I find myself checking my email when I'm supposed to be listening to my daughter. Then again, I am able to be with both of my children in the afternoons and we have so many experiences together that I would miss out on if I did not have the flexibility that a solo practice provides."
—**Stephanie Kimbro (class of 2003)**

"[Solo'ing as a single parent] is great. I still have to worry about my clients, but they don't care when and how I get the work done as long as it gets done. So, I drop my kids off at school and then work from 9 to 3. I pick them up and do the family thing until their bedtime. After that I usually put in a couple more hours. Night is actually an ideal time to do research or draft documents because there are fewer interruptions."
—**Lael Brown (class of 2009)**

10. How do you balance parenting with a solo practice?

"I was a single parent for 20 years while my kids were growing up. I had absolutely NO help from my ex in managing my daughter's college costs; it was all on me. [Being a single parent] was part of the reason I stayed so long in my government job. And I don't how I could [have ever solo'd] without my government pension and retired employee health insurance to support my daughter at the end of her last year of college. Even more stress-inducing than my parental obligation, though, is my involvement in the lives of my elderly parents, [one of whom] has Alzheimer's. It's a HUGE distraction from my legal work. I try to put it in the background, but it's not easy."
—**Jan M. Tamanini (class of 1984)**

11. What practice skills were you least prepared for?

"I was least prepared for court procedures. Law school did not teach me about local judges, how and where to file things, nor the importance of building relationships with court personnel. I had to learn all of this on the job."
—**Tonya Coles (class of 2006)**

"[Least prepared for]? The run-of-the-mill procedural stuff; the stuff they don't teach you in law school. Also, I had no idea how time-consuming it would be to track bills, deductions, expenses etc. Seems like that's half the job. It reminds me what a mentor told me: 'Spencer, start solo'ing when you're young. If I had learned how to run the business aspect of solo'ing at your age, I'd be a millionaire now.'"
—**Spencer Young (class of 2004)**

"As a new solo, I was least prepared for filing procedures even though I worked in the court system as a law student and immediately after graduating. Every court has its own system for filing and requires different forms to be filled. The only way to learn the procedures is to do them. Law school teaches you how to do legal research and writing, and how to think like a lawyer . . . but it does not teach you how to file a motion."
—**Adam Neufer (class of 2009)**

"[Least prepared for]? Doing the books. You have to constantly stay on top of it or you lose control of your money, and not know how much you are making v. spending. Now, I save every receipt and make sure everything is entered in QuickBooks. I spend a lot of time on [accounting], because it lets me know where I'm profiting and where I'm losing money. Until you review your QuickBooks reports, you will be surprised at some of the things draining money from your firm."
—**Paul Scott (class of 2008)**

"[Least prepared for]? Motion practice. Motions. Motions. Motions. The heart of family court."
—**Lynda L. Hinkle (class of 2009)**

"I lacked the practical skills; the administrative, accounting, and billing side of the practice. They had always been handled by the firm manager, and I didn't know how to do much of it."
—**Stephanie Kimbro (class of 2003)**

"Screening cases and setting retainers."
—**Nina Kallen (class of 1994)**

"Just how to draft a darn pleading. I made constant trips to the library to look up and copy pertinent pleadings."
—**Thomas J. Crane (class of 1983)**

"Discovery. I had worked for a litigation firm prior to going solo, but the paralegals always did all the discovery work. Since I couldn't afford my own help at the time, I had to figure out all the formatting and technical issues related to discovery questions, responses, subpoenas, notices, etc. A lot of this I couldn't find in CEB or Lexis. Luckily, I had a legal secretary friend who helped me out."
—**Lael Brown (class of 2009)**

"State court filings. I had never practiced in state court, and the inability to file electronically, combined with the arcane and unnecessarily complex rules, made it very difficult and time-consuming. I also had no experience with accounting or billing, but fortunately the software I ended up with (after a four-month false start with a program I ended up ditching) was sufficiently intuitive that I figured it out."
—**Mitchell J. Matorin (class of 1993)**

"The first time I solo'ed, the skills I was the least prepared for were depositions. I had never attended a deposition much less taken one, and I had no idea what I was doing! I also had never gone to court, and had to call up lots of seasoned practitioners to find out the 'rules of the game', especially for my first summary judgment motion."—**D. Jill Pugh (class of 1994)**

"I understood the laws, but I was unfamiliar with the actual practice and procedure of Criminal Law and the fact that it is different in every courtroom you step into."—**Jenee Oliver (class of 2005)**

"[For me], the actual practice of law was a challenge in the beginning. How and when to file motions or knowing the time schedules was difficult." —**Gabriel Cheong (class of 2007)**

"Law school prepared me to take the bar exam, but it did not prepare me for the business of law. I soon found that the fastest way to [learn] how to file a probate or record a deed is to go down to the courthouse, find a clerk in the appropriate office and say, "I'm a new attorney, how should I do/prepare/order/file _____ so that it makes your job easier?" After that, just fill in the blanks . . . and don't forget to send a note of thanks to the clerk." —**Bruce Cameron (class of 2007)**

"I was very prepared for the business side of law; the accounting, bookkeeping, marketing, the management of clients and employees, case load, and I had an intimate understanding of the bottom line. [What I wasn't prepared for] was figuring out proper venue and jurisdiction. I had no idea how to actually file the paper with the clerk of court's office, and I didn't know how to properly request service—either in the sheriff's office or on a petition. . . . " —**Scott Wolfe (class of 2005)**

11. What practice skills were you least prepared for?

"I've been a lawyer for about 10 years, but I've always worked for firms. I have no experience marketing or operating a law firm, and I was not prepared for marketing and practice management. I have been teaching myself through reading and trial and error, and I'm making good progress. But I have a long way to go."
—**Mark Tanney (class of 1998)**

"I still haven't figured out how someone learns how to handle a case in litigation. What's even more frightening is that, when asked, two very experienced litigators had very different answers to a simple question. I'm getting the impression no one really knows how to handle a case, and that there's no real right way. So, you just do what you can and hope for the best. I haven't had this confirmed yet, so take [this advice] with a grain of salt." —**Gina Bongiovi (class of 2007)**

"I felt pretty well-prepared [to solo] because I would prepare my case or matter, and then connect with a colleague who had been practicing much longer and review my preparation to be sure I hadn't missed any details. Networking is vitally important if you're a new lawyer with a solo practice. Its value cannot be overestimated."
—**Abbe W. McClane (class of 2003)**

"If you're in a law firm now and thinking of going solo, my advice is to learn the tasks that are now performed by your secretary since they may soon be performed by you."
—**Kevin Afghani (class of 2004)**

12. What was your most difficult client experience, and what did you learn?

"The worst clients are always the ones your gut tells you to run from at the start but you don't listen." —**Lynda L. Hinkle (class of 2009)**

"The worst client is the one who comes to you with a crisis, steals your heart and you agree to help them for a small down payment with the rest coming later . . . and then you don't get paid. The best client is the one willing to take their case to the end, is not overly emotional, and has a good case." —**Spencer Young (class of 2004)**

"I had one client who begged me to defend him against an ex parte motion scheduled for the next day. I agreed to do it, worked all night, and then won the motion. Then the client's check bounced and he declared bankruptcy. Now I only do work after a check has cleared. If it's an emergency I demand a cashier's check." —**Nina Kallen (class of 1994)**

"My worst client experience is happening right now. I took on a case several years ago, and my client became delinquent in his payments. I felt sorry for the client, and took his case all the way to the court of appeals without a proper retainer. I do not ever expect to be paid for my services."
—**Marc W. Matheny (class of 1980)**

"My worst client was a very needy man who had a case slightly outside of my area of expertise. He was very angry and emotionally exhausting. I knew the area of the law, and if I'd had time to really work the case I believe I would have got him a very good result. But we spent too much time fighting. He paid his bills, so I kept him on. Finally, after our third 'you-need-to-work-with-me-better' conversation, I fired him. After him, I listen when an inner voice tells me that someone will be hard to work with. It's just not worth the stress."
—**Matthew G. Kaiser (class of 2002)**

"My worst client was someone who used me as a doormat and attack dog. I'm not quite sure how he managed to get both out of me but he did. The client was one of the few exceptions I made to my payment-up-front rule and I got burned, and was someone who set off my BS detector though I refused to listen to it. He sucked a lot of my time with unnecessary (and unbilled) drama, refused to listen to my advice, and even attached letters I'd written to a threatening e-mail he sent to the opposing party! I finally had to rein him in. [Lesson learned]: never (EVER) deviate from my payment-up-front policy, listen to my BS detector when it's sounding like an air raid siren, and rein in a drama queen at the very beginning of the engagement."
—**Gina Bongiovi (class of 2007)**

"My worst client was a divorce client. In the months leading up to trial, the client ran out of money to replenish his retainer and I didn't get paid. However, I made the decision to go forward because I wasn't going to have many chances of bringing a divorce case to trial. So I basically traded my fees for the experience of trial. At the end of the day, I believe it was worth it because I learned a lot from practice that I wouldn't have reading from a trial textbook. After my experience, though, I never again had an outstanding balance on legal fees. That is because I have since started collecting flat fees for all divorces. I currently have no receivables, and all my legal fees are paid up-front." —**Gabriel Cheong (class of 2007)**

"My most difficult client had unreasonable expectations and refused to cooperate or compromise. He had created his own reality about his situation, and could not be reasoned with. It taught me the importance of a thorough intake process. There are a lot of questions I should have asked during the initial consultation, and had I been a little more thorough I might have saved myself a lot of trouble!"
—**Adam Neufer (class of 2009)**

"The worst clients were a very demanding business owner couple who had been casual friends. I allowed them to take advantage of that friendship to get a lot of free work. We had a fee agreement, but when I finally told them I would have to charge for services they made no payment for months and ignored my bills until I got insistent. It ended the friendship. What I learned is that they weren't friends I needed to have in my life." —**Jan M. Tamanini (class of 1984)**

"My worst client was my first; she was an unbelievable nightmare. She lied to me (and most others), she was erratic, uncooperative, verbally abusive, consumed an obscene amount of my time, and ended up owing me over $20,000 in legal fees. Needless to say, I learned an incredible amount: I grew much stronger and more assertive with respect to charging appropriate fees, and insisting on being paid . . . I became much more detailed in my Retainer Agreements and other correspondence, as well as how I structured the retainer amounts and my billing . . . and I learned quite a bit about certain areas of the law that my clients antics forced me to research. There were many valuable lessons."
—**Laura S. Mann (class of 1996)**

"My worst client experience occurred one year into practice. I was hired to complete an estate plan and halfway into my completing it the client decided not to proceed. She became extremely irate when I explained that I had earned some of her fee and that I would be returning her fee minus what I had earned. I learned from that experience that communication is key to client satisfaction. I now know that I must explain every detail of the legal services contract with each client, and that I must keep in regular contact with each client as I move forward with their legal matter." —**Tonya Coles (class of 2006)**

"My worst client was my first. It was a non-litigation matter, and I had offered him a choice of hourly or fixed fee and he chose fixed. The client turned out to be extremely demanding and required constant hand-holding, and did a lot of things on his own that made things unnecessarily complex. I finally lost my patience and told him he should find another attorney. Lesson learned: sometimes you have to fire a client to stay in business . . . and it's OK to do that. My other clients have all been great . . . with one exception: after two years of litigation, I was faced with a client with a huge balance who, while he didn't actually 'lose', he didn't 'win' either. Lesson learned: don't let your humanity and eagerness to help out make you lose sight of the fact that you have your own bills and your own family to feed." —**Mitchell J. Matorin (class of 1993)**

"My worst client was one who lied to me from the beginning about the car accident at issue. When confronted, the client still wouldn't admit it. When I asked to withdraw, the client would not agree to let me withdraw by stipulation. I had to bring a motion for $70, and drive four hours in order to be released from the case. The client refused to reimburse me for all of the costs I had spent on the client's case. I learned that I should trust my instincts when dealing with people's character and truthfulness." —**Brian T. Pedigo (class of 2007)**

"My clients have taught me that I am in the customer service business, and that there are no best/worst clients out there. While there may be situations where I am unable to fulfill all of a client's needs, it is not their fault that I failed to set or define their expectations properly. The upside is that each client is an opportunity to do better. This is not to say that there aren't difficult clients, clients who need hand-holding, or clients I would rather not have taken on. The typical client comes to me during times of stress. They are not in a frame of mind where they can operate at their highest, most rational self. The key is to remember that, in most cases, this is not what this client is really like, nor is this behavior intentionally directed at you." —**Bruce Cameron (class of 2007)**

"The most important thing I've learned about both good and bad client experiences is the importance of communication, and taking responsibility for anything that belongs with me." —**Cailie A. Currin (class of 1988)**

"I have had clients lie or conveniently forget to tell you something. I have since learned to ask anything and everything, and I watch them closely. It's a skill I learned conducting depositions for years in auto injury litigation. A facial expression can tell me there's more to the story, and that I have to keep probing. My favorite client has come to my house and helped with drywall. Who wouldn't love that?" —**Kara O'Donnell (class of 1995)**

12. **What was your most difficult client experience, and what did you learn?**

How do you deal with difficult clients?

The clients from hell ... that assorted collection ranging from the high-maintenance and nutty to the downright nasty and insulting. They call too much; they bounce checks; they denigrate lawyers (and by association, you); they ignore your advice to their detriment; they refuse to pay bills; and they repeatedly threaten to grieve you. As one management expert describes: Your worst clients are destroying your business. They demand 80 percent of your time and energy, and produce only 20 percent of your profit. Sooner or later (hopefully, sooner) you will reach a point where you must fire these clients lest they ruin your practice or even your life.

Here are some tips for dealing with difficult clients:

Share your misery. You may think your client's antics are unique, but at least one of your colleagues has dealt with similar behavior ... or worse. Seek out other solos for advice on how to deal with your troublesome client.

Put everything in writing. There's always a chance a problem client may eventually file a grievance against you. So, as much as you may want to avoid dealing with this client, it's important all communications with them are put into writing. Here is where e-mail can make a difference. When the problem client calls, respond by e-mail.

Raise your rates. Let the relationship run its course by finishing up any remaining work and avoiding new matters. When you complete the final piece of work, send a termination letter along with a final invoice, stating that your representation has ended. If the client calls to retain you later, politely explain that you are not accepting new matters. Or, raise your rates significantly if you think that will make your dealings with the client any more palatable.

Withdrawal in active matters. When clients act up during a matter that promises to last awhile, take stronger steps to fire the client.

Be candid about payment. If you withdraw for nonpayment, remind the client that, like any professional service provider, you're entitled to payment when you render service. If you're dealing with clients who have the means to pay but choose not to, no further discussion is warranted; you're better off rid of them. As for the client who truly can't afford to pay you, explore payment by credit card, family loan, or having the client continue the case pro se. Stand firm in your decision to withdraw.

Send a termination letter and files. Once you withdraw from representing a client, send a short, polite letter acknowledging the end of your representation. For ongoing matters where the client will need to retain new counsel, include a copy of the client's file.

Don't get cynical. Don't let the client from hell sour your experience of solo practice. For every problem client, you will find dozens of model clients who pay their bills on time (with checks that don't bounce!), express gratitude for your service, refer you cases, treat you to fancy lunches, and even send you gifts at holiday time. Serving clients like these makes solo practice a rewarding experience, one you should not sacrifice because of a few bad apples.

"Don't do it unless your heart is in it. But if you do, get a mentor who is no more than 10 years out of law school. They can give you relevant, helpful advice." —**Jenee Oliver (class of 2005)**

"[What I would tell new grads] is that solo'ing may or may not be for them. They should work in different environments . . . and know themselves . . . before making the decision. And they shouldn't go solo by default (e.g., layoff) or do it for the money. Solo because you like the profession, have the guts, want to be your own boss, and can deal with the ramifications of that decision." —**Spencer Young (class of 2004)**

"Yes [a new grad can solo]. But you need the guts to trust yourself, the desire to get up every day and hustle, and the willingness to admit that you don't know as much as you thought you did." —**Bruce L. Dorner (class of 1977)**

"There are two diametrically opposed schools of thought [about] solo'ing right out of law school. For myself, I feel it was important that I had a good grounding in the substantive law via work experience, practice skills, and practice management, before I went solo. I'm sure I'd have made many more mistakes if I'd gone solo right from law school, and would have missed out on some excellent experiences. Others feel that a new grad can go solo . . . but I believe that it's much harder." —**David Abeshouse (class of 1982)**

"In any business, you have four kinds of people: those who find the work, those who maintain client goodwill, those who make sure the work gets done, and those who actually do the work. If you don't have the personality to do all four, forget being a solo." —**Anonymous**

"Yes [you can solo right out of law school], but I recommend against it. New graduates know a lot of law (maybe more than they ever will again), but law school doesn't teach anything about having employees, running a business, or negotiating with vendors." —**Dean N. Alterman (class of 1989)**

"You can't just graduate from law school and expect to go to Staples and pick up the 'Start-Your-Own-Law-Firm' kit. It takes work, ingenuity, and sacrifice. [I suggest you] put yourself on the assigned counsel list (through the public defender) so you can take on cases that you know you will get paid for . . . take on wills or basic contracts you can do for a flat fee . . . work out of your living room . . . meet clients in coffee shops or at their homes. Be creative, and try to make ends meet." —**Anonymous**

"You will probably work harder as a solo than working for someone else! If you don't have the drive and courage necessary to be a business owner, you will not succeed. Building a law practice is not a Field of Dreams: if you just build it, they [clients] will not come. You need to be able to practice law AND be a great business owner and marketer at the same time." —**Gabriel Cheong (class of 2007)**

"If you think you might want to solo, go for it now (or early in your career), before the golden handcuffs go on." —**Anonymous (class of 1993)**

"Be prepared for the fear . . . market like crazy when business is slow . . . stay in contact with everyone you meet . . . don't be a general practitioner unless you're in a small town . . . and keep your expenses low. Be honest with yourself; not everyone is cut out to have their own practice. You'll be miserable if you try to be a business owner when you might be happiest as an employee." —**Gina Bongiovi (class of 2007)**

"Ask yourself why you want to solo. Who are you benefiting? If you say the client, you are fooling yourself. What experience are you bringing to the table to help the client? And if you say you don't want to work for the 'man', think about whether you want to be a lawyer. Lawyering is not a free-wheeling crusade; a lawyer represents a client, and has a time-honored duty to zealously represent the client's interest within ethical and legal boundaries." —**Herb Dubin (class of 1964)**

"The hardest thing is the decision whether to go solo. It was for me. Sometimes people can get hung up on over-planning. It's kind of like the decision about whether to have a baby: probably you would never do it if you waited until all the ducks were in a row. There are some things you just can't plan for, and you just need to figure it out as you go." —**Adam Neufer (class of 2009)**

"If you want to solo, you need to be a businessperson first and a lawyer second. You need to know budgets and finance; you need to know advertising and marketing; you need to know cost-analysis; you need to be able to differentiate yourself from the other lawyers and sell that difference to the community. And you need to supply good product, stay within your expertise, and be there when your clients and prospective clients need you." —**Anonymous**

"[As new grads], you will meet more naysayers than you can imagine who will tell you all of the downsides to being a solo. [But] you will be more successful if you can learn who to listen to . . . and who to ignore. Do your own research; think for yourself. If you can't do that, then don't be

surprised when you find yourself spending years bored and uninspired working for someone else, and building their dream instead of your own. If you can get through those first few years [of solo practice], the long-term rewards are worth all the risk and fear at the beginning."
—**Stephanie Kimbro (class of 2003)**

"Don't expect to make much money for the first two to three years of practice!"
—**Brian T. Pedigo (class of 2007)**

"I think one can [solo right out of law school], but it would be so much harder. There is so much valuable information learned through working that can make the solo choice easier. But . . . if someone is dedicated to the [solo] path and works hard at it, it can be done."
—**Cailie A. Currin (class of 1988)**

"I did it. You can, too. Limit your practice area to something with which you are familiar and that you enjoy. I would also tell [new grads] that the struggles of solo practice are no worse or better than the struggles of any other type of practice just different. If you prefer to be your own boss, you will certainly trade that aspect for a smaller or less regular income. But if money is vitally important to your well-being; if a regular paycheck is a must, then solo practice is not for you."
—**Marc W. Matheny (class of 1980)**

"I wouldn't recommend [soloing] fresh out of school. A new grad doesn't have the experience and knowledge to be effective. Most successful solos I know have 5-10 years big firm or government experience." —**A Houston solo**

"Consider spending at least a couple of years with a law firm to learn the fundamentals of practicing

law in the areas you seek, and learn the day-to-day operations and management of a law firm."
—**Brian M. Annino (class of 2003)**

"[What would I tell new grads about solo'ing]? That it's worth it. But first you need to get some experience, unless you've grown up in the city where you plan to solo, and where you have family who already practice law there. My having done defense work for five years first helped a great deal with networking and name recognition."
—**Michael Moebes (class of 2003)**

"Unless you're extremely well-connected in law school, I don't know how a new law school graduate could have a client or contact base that would allow him/her to pay down their student loans. For me, going the law firm route enabled me to significantly pay down my student loans and other obligations to allow for the risk that comes with going solo. If you do choose to solo, consider project-partnering with an experienced lawyer in your practice area. They will be able to provide you with referrals and the mentoring you need. Of course, they will also probably require you to share fees with them, but this sacrifice could yield long-term benefits. I recommend partnering with an attorney who allows you to have direct contact with clients for which you perform the work."
—**Kevin Afghani (class of 2004)**

"For some practice areas, a new attorney fresh out of law school can do fine (I'm thinking criminal defense, for example, where you can get on a bar counsel list and at least have some guaranteed clients and get some experience completely apart from marketing and business generation). For other areas, that's more difficult. You just can't waltz out of law school into a business litigation practice and expect to succeed in the short term;

law school doesn't teach you how to practice law. Clients need to know that you have experience, and they are usually not eager to be your guinea pig. And then there is your ethical obligation to your clients to represent them competently. You can't do that if you don't even know what questions need asking, or what steps need to be taken. If you must solo [without legal experience] —or if you have always felt that this is what you want to do —go for it. But if you have the option of working in a firm for a few years, do that instead. You'll see how things are really done, and that will translate into self-confidence that you actually can do it." —**Mitchell J. Matorin (class of 1993)**

"It is certainly possible to hang your shingle right out of law school, but it would be better to get a few years of experience. Not necessarily legal experience; instead, experience in the inner workings of a law firm work: how to create files, how correspondence should be saved, etc. If getting a few years experience is not possible, some law school internships could definitely achieve the same goal. And if that is not possible, go to a lot of CLE's on law practice management."
—**Paul Scott (class of 2008)**

"I imagine it would be difficult to do. My only prior legal experience is the 2 1/2 years as a law clerk, and I learned a lot during that time. I couldn't imagine going solo without that experience. Also, I have a decade of experience as an office manager/account manager which helps me with all the other aspects of running my own office. I would recommend that a new attorney at least have some kind of experience running an office if nothing else, or hire help right off the bat. An experienced legal secretary can be worth his or her weight in gold —especially for a newbie."
—**Lael Brown (class of 2009)**

"The biggest struggle and frustration for me is finding clients. I expect that most new attorneys will also find this to be a big challenge. Starting a solo practice is a large undertaking, all the more so for a newly licensed attorney. Some new attorneys have been able to pull it off, but I would say you should think thrice about it, especially if you have large student loans. The key ingredient is a burning desire to go solo. If you have that, you have a good chance to succeed."
—**Mark Tanney (class of 1998)**

"[My advice]? Have a slush fund for the first two to three months. Do doc review if you have nothing in your bank account. Intern if you have to. Just get experience, and always be hungry for the next opportunity. You never know where it will lie. Just don't quit even when business gets slow even if it is slow for two months! Also, consider interning for free with an attorney if you have to. Just get experience some way, somehow."
—**Kara O'Donnell (class of 1995)**

"Have a mentor or two. Don't try to spread yourself across multiple practice areas. Focus on one and become competent in that field before adding additional practice areas. Attend all the CLE's in your practice area that you can afford; they're a great way to learn the in-and-out of your practice area, and a great place to find mentors and to network. Have faith in yourself. If you weren't competent to practice law, the Court would not have granted you your license. Don't rush out and get that subscription to Westlaw or Lexis. Learn to use the free research services out there. If you absolutely have to have access to a pay site, consider joining the Jenkins Law Library; you get 30 minutes per day of Lexis access as part of the membership."
—**Bruce Cameron (class of 2007)**

"Make friends with more experienced attorneys in your practice areas. Take them to lunch and show your gratitude. Every experienced attorney I've met has been more than willing to help out a newbie, but be sure you don't take advantage. Find some CLE courses to supplement your knowledge, and don't take on any client you can't handle. In the beginning, you'll feel like you can't handle anything, but the trick is not to commit to representing the client during the consultation. Tell them you have to review the file before committing. Then go home, research the bejeezus out of whatever issue they have, and figure out if you can take it. Most of the time, you'll find you don't have the answers, but you know where to go to get them. That's what counts."
—**Gina Bongiovi (class of 2007)**

"[My advice]: network, network. Get to know everybody. Once you're done networking, network some more. Volunteer your time, because it's a 'giver's gain.' But if you do volunteer, follow through with everything. You'll prove yourself as a professional, and other professionals will respond to that quickly." —**Eric P. Ganci (class of 2008)**

"Go for it . . . but do this first: talk to three solo lawyers to get a sense for different perspectives, ideas, struggles; think about how to keep your overhead low at the start, and create a business plan that includes a mission statement and a SWOT analysis. I would also tell [new grads] that starting out you will feel that your efforts are not working . . . you will reach out to people for work and referrals, and it will feel that nothing came of the effort . . . and you will place advertisements and it will seem as if no one sees them. But, eventually, you will see a steady stream of business, and realize that all of your hard work early on did pay off." —**Tonya Coles (class of 2006)**

"[What would I tell new grads]? Some of the positives [about solo'ing] can also be negatives. Yes, you can make your own hours. But if you do make your own hours, you also have to make them up, too. Yes, you can take an afternoon off to play golf, but you'll be going in over the weekend or holiday to catch up. And, yes, you are the boss . . . but you're also the one who has

to take the heat for the workload. And, yes, you benefit from all the profits . . . but you alone bear any loss."
—**Abbe W. McClane (class of 2003)**

"If you try [solo'ing] but you don't like it . . . move on. Nothing has to be forever."
—**Nina Kallen (class of 1994)**

How to lay the groundwork in law school

Whether you want to start a firm right out of law school or several years later, there are many steps you can take during law school to ease the transition and maximize your chances of success:

Financial management. If you're a law student, lenders will tempt you with extra loans to subsidize unpaid summer jobs or to help cover costs while you study for the bar. Don't go for it. Instead, spend time with an online calculator (e.g., www.edfed.com/resources/calculators.php) to help you figure out your post-law school month debt payments, and to understand what your monthly repayment options will look like as you take on extra debt.

Course selection. Virtually every law school offers a variety of practical training in the second and third year. And most law schools have clinics for hands-on experience in advising clients, drafting complaints and briefs, and arguing cases in court. While you're at it, load up on skills-related classes: negotiation, trial practice, contract drafting, legal writing.

Work experience. Some law schools offer internship programs where students can seek

placement in positions at legal aid clinics, judge's offices, or in-house at corporations. Some solo-bound students make the mistake of ignoring internships because they're unpaid, and rarely provide the chance to work in a solo or small firm office. But there's a great deal of value to the contacts that you make in any internship position, and they will serve you well if you do start your own firm.

Adjuncts. Most law school faculties employ experienced practitioners as adjunct professors. Make them your best friends! Most of the lawyers who serve as adjuncts can offer valuable career advice or possibly introduce you to potential contacts.

Online outreach. Both the Internet and social media give law students extraordinary access to mentors and contacts outside the confines of the law school. Join listservs like the ABA's Solosez to learn more about solo practice, and to get to know other solo lawyers in the community.

"[My biggest goof was] challenging a judge's ruling on a point of law that I knew absolutely NOTHING about. I was winging it at a hearing for a client, and I asked the judge why she was ruling against me on some issue. She tore me in half because it was obvious I had no idea what I was talking about. Hilarious and pathetic at the same time." —**Spencer Young (class of 2004)**

"Starting out, I wasted a lot of my savings on status things that I thought every law firm had to have in order to be legit. For example, I thought I had to have a listing at Lawyers.com for $2,000 a year in order to be 'found' by clients. Not true; there are better ways for solos to market themselves. I discovered organic SEO (search engine optimization) and about free, online social media."
—**Stephanie Kimbro (class of 2003)**

"My biggest mistake? I made some costly errors by not working with an accountant to set up my books initially. I should have used a more forgiving piece of software, and a course on accounting for small business would have been a much smarter way to go!" —**Cailie A. Currin (class of 1988)**

"The biggest goof I ever made was not hiring a full time receptionist/secretary earlier in my career."
—**Marc W. Matheny (class of 1980)**

"[Biggest goof]? Agreeing to represent the senior VP of a Fortune 50 company. Dealing with him on a daily and weekly basis, [he exhibited] what I gently call an aberrant personality (e.g., he was also a clever liar who covered his tracks well). I fired him about a week or two before I would have become official counsel of record, and chalked up several thousand dollars in unpaid legal fee to my practice management education. I vowed to scrutinize all

prospective clients even more carefully in future." —**David Abeshouse (class of 1982)**

"[Biggest goof]? Letting a client accrue a huge outstanding balance on a litigation matter that took a tremendous amount of my time (and many all-nighters). I let the empathy I felt for the client, who had to defend against a full-blown lawsuit over a dispute that easily should have settled, get in the way of good business sense. Although empathy is a good thing, when it comes to running a solo practice it has to be backed up with a somewhat cold-hearted view of the bottom line."
—**Mitchell J. Matorin (class of 1993)**

"I tried a case with my fly unzipped. I won."
—**Michael Moebes (class of 2003)**

"Early on, I failed to identify my ideal type of client, or focus my efforts on acquiring this ideal type of client. Instead, my business development efforts followed a scattershot approach. Lunches are a great way to meet with potential clients, but general and random lunches with people, while fun, really aren't as effective as strategically pursuing desirable clients. I realized I might be on the wrong track when the people with whom I met were telling me things like, 'I don't think I've ever met anyone who needed a patent.'"
—**Kevin Afghani (class of 2004)**

"As local counsel for an out-of-state attorney, I neglected to claim the arbitration exemption that applies to cases in excess of $50,000 IF you plead the exemption in the complaint. I ended up having to file a motion to exempt the case from arbitration and it was granted. Of course, I've only been practicing for three years so if that's my biggest goof I'll be in great shape."
—**Gina Bongiovi (class of 2007)**

14. What was your biggest goof, and what did it teach you?

"[Biggest goof]? Answering a call from the bankruptcy clerk at 8:30 in the morning, and sounding drunk because I had been working up until 3 a.m. No more late nights on weekdays! [From now on], I keep banker's hours despite my solo status." **—Kara O'Donnell (class of 1995)**

"My two biggest goofs —of equal proportion and equal bad consequence —were (a) failing to develop a second and third specialty [before my small, highly specialized firm was destroyed by the deregulation of the transportation industry], and (b) never learning about (and never asking about) marketing. Those goofs were never resolved." **—Herb Dubin (class of 1964)**

"I am constantly revising my retainer agreements to try to eliminate problems that rise from not being clear enough with clients about what happens when 'things come up'. Live and learn." **—Lynda L. Hinkle (class of 2009)**

"I'm primarily transactional-based. So far, none of my goofs have been made public yet!" **—Jeffrey G. Neu (class of 2006)**

15. What important issues do new solos face?

"[Important issues]? Learning that practicing law is a business, and that in addition to good legal skills, you can't lose sight of the need for adequate business records and procedures." **—Bruce L. Dorner (class of 1977)**

"I think financial issues are the hardest. Another very real challenge is making sure that the legal work done does not get compromised because of the competing demands of running a business and maintaining high quality work." **—Cailie A. Currin (class of 1988)**

"The first [issue] is money, not just the startup money but the cash flow. No one should start a solo practice without first budgeting the costs, and figuring out a target cash flow and expense projection." **—Dean N. Alterman (class of 1989)**

"A new or prospective solo should think carefully about the type of area that they want to practice. It is too difficult for a general practitioner to stand out as a 'go-to' person, and marketing is easier when there is a target audience. This is not to say that you need to limit yourself to taking only certain cases. But it is easier to sell yourself when you are more knowledgeable or experienced in a particular area. And the chance of being remembered—by neighbors, acquaintances, or just someone you meet at a networking function—is much higher if you have 'specialized'." **—Jenny Jeltes (class of 2006)**

"I think the biggest struggle is isolation. If you are a loner, I do not think you can truly succeed as a solo. You must have people with whom you can brainstorm, bounce ideas off, and ask for help. Certainly the Internet and listservs make this easier, but there is no substitution for human contact. Not only do you need it to build your referral base, you need it so you have a shoulder to cry on when a judge or a client does something really stupid!" —**D. Jill Pugh (class of 1994)**

"A lot of people think that going solo means a better work schedule because you're in charge. But you [often] end up working longer harder than you would at a firm. To go solo, you must be honest about who you are. If you know you're not disciplined enough to make your own schedule, manage myriad deadlines, and be proactive about growing your business, perhaps you shouldn't solo." —**Adam Neufer (class of 2009)**

"[Ask yourself] if you have the personality to be a business owner. No one can tell you if you will succeed, but only you know if you have the drive to succeed. You also need to also look at your [finances]. How much money have you saved up, or how much can you borrow? On average, I would say that it takes at least nine months until you start breaking even from month to month."
—**Gabriel Cheong (class of 2007)**

"[Ask yourself] whether you are cut out for solo practice: the unpredictability, the autonomy, and being in charge of your own destiny and not having a supervisor over your shoulder. It isn't everyone's cup of tea. Be honest as to whether you'd be happier as an employee in a firm. A few months into my solo practice, I had a conversation with my husband who, in response to a stressed-out tantrum of mine asked me, 'Wouldn't you rather work for a firm?' No. I would gladly worry about the overhead, the administrative tasks, and all of that just to AVOID going to work and getting paid. [This way], I have no office politics, no one second-guessing my sick days, and no time-card to punch." —**Gina Bongiovi (class of 2007)**

"Take a long look at your finances before starting. If you have three young children, no savings, and $1,200 in monthly student loan payments, then starting a new law practice is going to be tough. It's still possible, just difficult. Beyond the financial issue, the key question goes to motivation: the key indicator of a solo's success is a true desire to solo. If you want to solo just to get through the downturn until jobs come back, [solo practice] may prove difficult." —**Mark Tanney (class of 1998)**

"Save enough money to last several months or more without income. And consider whether you're the type of person who would flip out if you had to go long stretches of watching your checking account diminish."
—**Kevin Afghani (class of 2004)**

"You need to have a good support network, and (considerable) savings to survive the slow times. Keep overhead low. Be choosy where you decide to invest your funds for building up the practice. And don't advertise. Most attorneys will tell you it doesn't pay off that well, and I found that to be true." —**Sergio Benavides (class of 2005)**

"A prospective solo should consider what kind of network they have available, and how they can make use of it. I started soloing in a community where I have lived for many years. I have many contacts through my extended family, my old work, my kids' school, my hobbies, my husband's work, etc. I use these contacts all the time. I couldn't imagine being successful without having this network. I don't think I would be as successful if I just opened shop in some random area."
—**Lael Brown (class of 2009)**

"You really have to make an effort to be involved with your business community. If you sit in a home office and wait for work to come to you, they'll be hauling your dust-covered skeleton out at the end. Maintain outside contacts with both friends and business associates; get out to networking events, volunteer with local groups (you may find great referrals from those efforts), and have lunch outside of your office on a regular basis. The isolation is something you really have to work to overcome. Also, focus on a few primary practice areas instead of trying to do everything. Don't accept cases you're not well-qualified to handle no matter how attractive they may look. That doesn't mean you can't do something that's not second-nature; it means you should know what you can easily research and work with as opposed to something too complicated and out of your comfort zone." —**Jan M. Tamanini (class of 1984)**

"[Ask yourself]: Is your spouse/significant other on board with your decision to solo? Do you have a support system? Who will you turn to for advice (legal and business)? Do you have a business plan? A marketing plan? A budget? Any idea of your client demographics? What if any statutory requirements or bar requirements are there for solos? Where will you practice? What about insurance (malpractice, liability, errors & omission coverage)? Do you even need insurance? Do you know how to do trust accounting? Do you even need a trust account? How will you fund your practice? My advise is to listen respectfully to the advice of those you respect, research those points that resonate with your concerns, and ignore the rest until you are forced to face them." —**Bruce Cameron (class of 2007)**

"[Ask yourself]: do I have a family to support? Do I have others dependent upon me who would suffer? Or am I better off working at the Legal Aid office part-time just to have some income coming in to the family?" —**Marc W. Matheny (class of 1980)**

"Every day is a risk. Every client is a risk. Every time you walk into court it's a risk. It's all risk, isn't it? What else is there but endless risk? [A solo practice is] not for the faint-hearted." —**Lynda L. Hinkle (class of 2009)**

"I feel like I'm gambling every day. The cases and clients I take have to be good because I am putting everything on the line for them. [To be a solo], you have to have a very high risk tolerance, one where you either 'make it or break it.'" —**Brian T. Pedigo (class of 2007)**

"Risk is an everyday thing for solos. You may have $100,000 'on the streets', and if you're not comfortable with managing that kind of debt —and if you don't have a pretty intimate understanding of how to deal with cash flow —you're going to be in one too many financial pinches to remain in business. Every dollar you put into a case —or into your firm's brand —is another dollar you're risking for the success of the firm." —**Scott Wolfe (class of 2005)**

"You have to be a risk-taker to own your own business … any business … but especially a law practice. In addition to cash-flow fluctuations, there is the added risk of malpractice claims by disgruntled clients." —**Traci D. Ellis (class of 1990)**

"The prospective solo has to be able to stomach a fair bit of risk, because you ultimately have only yourself to rely on. And that doesn't really change as long as you're a solo, although there are ways in which you can modify that effect over time by using outsourcing judiciously." —**David Abeshouse (class of 1982**

"Based on my experience, one of the most important personality traits of a solo practitioner is a high tolerance for risk. If you are uncomfortable with not getting paid for over a month or two, and not being able to accurately project your income —at least in the starting phase —you should think seriously about your decision to solo. Indeed, the risk factor is the main force preventing many of my colleagues from breaking out on their own. For example, one of the commonly cited reasons that my friends give me for not going out on their own is that there is no financial bottom as to how low they can be. They're correct, but some solos find this to be a strong source of motivation: when they sense their income is about to hit rock 'bottom', they double their efforts to get back in the black again. Getting a regular paycheck at law firm can be false sense of security, especially with [all] the layoffs. When you work for a law firm, your entire future can be in the hands of one or two partners, whereas in the solo situation, your livelihood often depends on many clients. The loss of one, while regrettable, is not fatal."
—**Kevin Afghani (class of 2004)**

"Risk and solo practice are synonymous. As rewarding as it is, solo practice is incredibly unpredictable and inherently risky. You bear the brunt of bad court decisions (especially in a contingency fee practice), and you bear the risk of clients who fail to pay."—**D. Jill Pugh (class of 1994)**

"Risk is the ever-present ghost over your shoulder. From month to month, you can't rely on a steady income. You don't know if your clients will pay; you don't know if the phone will ring; you don't know if any consultation will turn into a client; you don't know if your particular niche will be eliminated due to some new legislation. Risk is probably the biggest factor in a solo practice. The trick is to figure out how to manage it, strategically and emotionally, so that dips don't sideline you, and you don't overspend in the good months. Budgeting is a great tool, as is having a solid business plan that you revisit every few months to make sure you're on the right track."
—**Gina Bongiovi (class of 2007)**

"I think you feel risk much more as a solo practitioner. It is something that you are solely responsible for because anything that comes out of your practice is generated by your actions alone. It makes me extra careful when I'm drafting and reviewing what I send out to the client because I can't rely on staff to correct things. Regarding risk, I also find myself turning down projects much more as a solo where I feel like I may not have the competency in that area of the law to handle it without a mentor. In my old firm, I might have taken more risk by taking a case like that knowing that I would have other associates with experience in that area to draw from."
—**Stephanie Kimbro (class of 2003)**

"The role of risk will vary for each person. For example, if a solo attorney has money in the bank and a good book of business, the risk may not be that great; conversely, if the attorney is starting out with a minimal budget, no client base, and huge student loans, then the attorney will have a much greater risk. Other factors also play into the picture. If you are 30 years old and able to work a full time job while you start your practice, this may help reduce your risk. And if your spouse is willing and able to cover expenses until you get off the ground, that, too, will help reduce your risk. So the role of risk will vary."
—**Mark Tanney (class of 1998)**

16. **What role does risk play in a solo pratice?**

"[A solo's] risk isn't that much different from those borne by other practitioners . . . with one exception: it's all on you. There's no one else to take up the slack if you have a slow period or get sick. And if one of your clients has a crisis demanding big chunks of your time, you can't just let everything else slide. The best way I've found to manage this—and it's still a struggle for me—is to make sure I give myself more time than I think I'll need to complete a client project. If something should take a few days, I'll tell the client I'll get it done in ten days; if it should take a week, I'll tell the client two. That way, if you finish on your original estimate, the client thinks you're wonderful; if you have something else come up, and you take the longer time, the client isn't disappointed." **—Jan M. Tamanini (class of 1984)**

"[In my experience], going solo means spending large amounts of time and money in a venture with no defined return, and with odds that are undefined, unpredictable, and continuously variable! It's an intricate dance with risk . . . but not a gamble. [To manage risk], you need to think strategically, making decisions based on information and a cost/benefit analysis rather than reacting to immediate events. The fact that I could not predict all the possible risk involved in being solo was one of the biggest stumbling blocks I had when deciding to go solo. Now, risk is what makes my solo practice fun, exhilarating, worrisome . . . and scary at the same time. It's what keeps me sharp and drives me to do my best work."
—Bruce Cameron (class of 2007)

"Risk is a big factor in starting a solo practice, but risk is a factor in almost all decisions in life. The goal should not be to avoid risk, but to understand, mitigate, and manage it.

You have to be willing to risk your money, savings, and steady paycheck. But if you make a good business plan, stick to it, and can see how you are going to feed yourself, you are managing that risk. Before I started my solo practice, I spent hours and hours in front of Excel spreadsheets, figuring out how much income I would need for the practice to stay afloat, how much I needed to bring home, etc. I take the same approach with cases that I decide to take, marketing decisions, etc. There is always going to be a risk that you won't get a good return on your investment."
—Paul Scott (class of 2008)

"I [used to have] high anxiety whenever my firm's bank account was low. It was scary wondering what would happen month-to-month. After only nine months of being a solo, though, that anxiety is rarely an issue. [But] the other risk involves being able to do the legal task in a professional manner without the benefit of another attorney down the hall to bounce questions off. The only solution? Read . . . research . . . read more. Repeat." **—Kara O'Donnell (class of 1995)**

"As with most things, the greater the risk the greater the possibility of the reward. You might fail, but if you don't it'll be worth it. [And] even if you fail, you would've learned something from the failure and hopefully you'll do better next time. Attorneys are by nature, risk-adverse. However, if you took the step to start a law practice, you're already willing to take more risk than other attorneys. [My advice]: just go with it."
—Gabriel Cheong (class of 2007)

"For me the biggest challenge is getting clients. I feel fine about everything else."
—**Mark Tanney (class of 1998)**

"Making money. Getting clients. Knowing your field of law. Never stop reading in your field."
—**Kara O'Donnell (class of 1995)**

"Maintaining regular cash flow over the long haul, and not spending the money before you collect it."
—**Bruce L. Dorner (class of 1977)**

"How to budget and how to read financial statements. No one should start and run a business who cannot read financial statements. And the next [challenge] is in understanding the difference between cash and accrual accounting; you can't eat accounts receivable."
—**Dean N. Alterman (class of 1989)**

"[Biggest challenge]? Managing the schedule, making sure there is enough work to pay the bills, and keeping on top of all the administrative tasks. I work a lot of hours to make sure it all gets done."—**Jeffrey G. Neu (class of 2006)**

"Having to do everything myself. I cope by organizing things to death. Each day is calendared, scheduled, prioritized. If I have to make a trip to the courthouse, I schedule it when I have several cases to work on there. I return client and business calls while driving. And if necessary, I go in early and stay late... and I'm no stranger to weekend work." —**Abbe W. McClane (class of 2003)**

"[The biggest challenge when you're the boss]? You're not just the boss . . . you're the secretary, the IT department, the marketing department, the CPA, and everything else!"
—**Jenee Oliver (class of 2005)**

"[As the boss] you need to establish a budget for insurance (health, dental, malpractice, disability), and any of the other services normally provided by an employer. Second, set up a time management and appointment system, because you will have to wear many different hats on any given day, including collector, lawyer, accountant, PR expert, or janitor. [Having a system in place] helps to ensure that your highest priorities are always addressed. Third, talk to a CPA, and keep an organized file for any records that may be required by the IRS, including business receipts and income statements."
—**Kevin Afghani (class of 2004)**

"Time management is one of the biggest challenges. The trouble is not in making sure that filing deadlines are met, or that the statute of limitations has not expired, or even making sure that you make client meetings on time. The trouble is in avoiding time sinks; that oh-I'll-just-spend-a-few-more-minutes-researching-this, or, 'I only need a couple of moments for this blog entry to be perfect, or I'll take a quick break here and write a bill or two', or even let a client meeting stretch out another 10 minutes. These, 'oh-it's-just-a-minute-or-two's' can eat hours out of an otherwise productive day. The only defense is to schedule everything, and to stick to that schedule religiously." —**Bruce Cameron (class of 2007)**

"My biggest day-to-day challenges fall into the balancing category: family/work; doing the work myself/having paralegal staff do the work; doing billable work/doing marketing and business work. And there are never enough hours in the day for all of it. As it is, I generally work 10-12 hours a day, and never feel like I got everything done that I wanted to."—**Cailie A. Currin (class of 1988)**

"Budget, budget, and . . . budget! Budget your time so you don't dawdle over pointless stuff and let the important things get away. Budget your resources in the most cost-efficient way possible. And budget your energies so you can do everything you have to do without burning out. It took some time to [learn how to] do this, and every now and then I still let one of my budgets get out of balance." **—Jan M. Tamanini (class of 1984)**

"[My biggest challenges]? 1) Fees. Deciding how much to charge in fixed fees, and which clients to turn away. I changed my fixed-fees several times until I finally figured out what my time was worth and what my clients could pay. 2) Office administration. I was not familiar with this side of the practice, so I had an accountant teach me how software could track items for tax purposes. 3) Self-confidence. There are still dry spells in my business, and I have doubts that it will come back. I cope by maintaining the online support networks (primarily Twitter and Solosez), and chatting and listening to other solos going through the same situations." **—Stephanie Kimbro (class of 2003)**

"[For me, the three biggest challenges] are a) working too much, b) working too little, and c) getting complacent about marketing. Working too much? It sounds silly, but I get so engrossed in work that I forget to eat until my head starts to throb. Now, I set a timer. Working too little? There are days where I want nothing more than to turn the alarm off and go back to sleep, but I make sure to schedule myself something to do each day so that I don't get lazy. Getting complacent on marketing? Some days I think if I have to attend one more rubber-chicken luncheon, I might punch someone's lights out. But then I remember that the people I met three months ago are only now starting to retain me, and I don't want to take a

week off and then have a dead week three months from now. [As a solo], you just have to constantly fill the funnel with contacts in the hopes that a small percentage of those contacts will fall out of the funnel as clients."
—Gina Bongiovi (class of 2007)

"[The biggest challenges] are deciding which expenditures are worthwhile during the first few months. I bought used [office] furniture and good technology on sale. [Another challenge] is learning how to 'unplug' when you're away from the office. I still can't do this; even on vacation in Costa Rica, I checked email and voicemail!"
—Michael Moebes (class of 2003)

"Challenge #1: Get the right staff. I was extremely lucky in that I had three excellent secretaries over the years, all of whom have worked virtually full-time for part-time wages. For those few months in which I did not have those secretaries, I went through at least 10 staff. Challenge #2: Don't [envy] the other guy. It is too easy to say the grass is greener on the other side of the fence. Look at what you have, and why you chose to start your own practice; then evaluate whether you are better off. I always end up feeling pretty good about my life." **—Marc W. Matheny (class of 1980)**

"Most of the time I like the autonomy of a solo practice. There are times when I wish there was another attorney to shoulder some of the load, but most often I am very happy to be the one who does the day-to-day work and who gets to make the strategic decisions."
—**Cailie A. Currin (class of 1988)**

"[I like the autonomy], but the ease of having a colleague down the hall to bounce ideas around is something I miss from my earlier days. [As a solo], you have to make a point to pick up the phone and arrange a time to talk, or better yet, a time to meet in person. Too much online and phone contact without face time can make you a little stir crazy."
—**Jan M. Tamanini (class of 1984)**

"I love not having to answer to anybody other than my client (and the Court), but I miss the ability to walk next door and bend somebody's ear on an issue." —**Mitchell J. Matorin (class of 1993)**

"I miss having co-workers. Sometimes I feel like the Tom Hanks character [in the movie Castaway], talking to a volleyball when he was marooned on an island in the Pacific."
—**Kara O'Donnell (class of 1995)**

"I enjoy the freedom of running my business as I decide, but it would be nice to have another attorney close by with whom to discuss cases and situations." —**Abbe W. McClane (class of 2003)**

"I like that, for the most part, I get to decide which cases to take. I also like the fact that I am the sole face of my practice, and that its image depends entirely on my efforts. My least favorite aspect of solo-ing is the isolation. It would be nice to have another attorney to run ideas by."
—**Adam Neufer (class of 2009)**

"[I love the autonomy]. I can sneak out early when I can, or stay late when I have to."
—**Thomas J. Crane (class of 1983)**

"I love the autonomy [of being a solo]. It means being able to take care of a friend after surgery, being able to attend my nephew's basketball game, being able to take my dog to the vet."
—**Gina Bongiovi (class of 2007)**

"I like traveling a lot. As a solo, no one tells me I can't pick that CLE in Maui or Vancouver as they did when I did defense work."
—**Michael Moebes (class of 2003)**

"It's great having the freedom to set my own schedule. The downside is that I start to set my schedule for the convenience of my clients by opening early, staying late, or having weekend hours. It's great for clients, but it cuts into time with my family. I know there is a solution, but I feel guilty taking time off or even shorting my working hours; it feels a bit like I am abandoning my baby. The other thing about a solo's autonomy is that I have the office space to myself; I can bring my dogs and/or parrot into work, I can turn up the volume on my favorite music, and I can wander the halls muttering without worrying that someone will be concerned for my sanity. The downside is that there's no one to have lunch with (the dogs aren't big on conversation)."
—**Bruce Cameron (class of 2007)**

"The only thing I dislike [about the autonomy of a solo practice] is the financial aspect. I cannot afford the best case management software. I cannot afford the extra staff to help in the office. And I cannot afford new furniture for my office. Fortunately, I share a building full of other lawyers so there is always another lawyer to go to discuss

case issues or just knock ideas around. When I was a true solo, all alone in my own office, it was much more difficult to relate ideas and issues with lawyers outside the office."
—**Marc W. Matheny (class of 1980)**

"I love the autonomy [of solo practice] because I hate being told what to do, and I hate having to compromise my values or my ideals. [The downside of autonomy] is that sometimes I get guilted into taking a smaller [fee] than I should from a client, and I wish I had someone around who would [point that out]. I am learning to let go of that guilt, and just do what I need to do for my business."—**Lynda L. Hinkle (class of 2009)**

"I'm an entrepreneur, and solo practice feeds that part of my personality. I am also a bit of an introvert, and being able to work on my own—in the way that I work —is ideal. The only thing I dislike about the autonomy is that the risk is all on my shoulders."—**Stephanie Kimbro (class of 2003)**

"Yes, having your own firm means you get to make your own schedule for the most part, and pick your own clients, and be your own boss. It also means that you reap what you sow; there is no steady paycheck, no one to make decisions for you, and having to work harder than if you were an employee." —**Gabriel Cheong (class of 2007)**

"In my opinion, the challenges of being solo are far outweighed by the benefits. I enjoy figuring out, or verifying, things on my own instead of taking other people's word for it. I respond better to situations in which self-motivation is required, as opposed to control methods from a superior. And I enjoy having control of my own destiny, instead of having my future determined by a handful of partners who may or may not

have a real interest in my future growth. The autonomy of being solo means pushing your skill set in directions you never thought you'd need as a lawyer. For someone who enjoys constant challenge in a variety of different arenas, starting and running your own practice could provide the challenge you need."
—**Kevin Afghani (class of 2004)**

"What autonomy? Autonomy as a solo is a fiction. Clients make unfair, unreasonable, irrational demands, and so does the legal system, i.e., judges. At least in a small or big firm, sharing the burden of such demands gives you the autonomy to plan your personal life."
—**Herb Dubin (class of 1964)**

"My biggest frustration as a solo is the same I've had since Day 1: no steady stream of revenue, no regular paycheck, and I never know from one month to the next what will be coming in."
—**Marc W. Matheny (class of 1980)**

"[My frustrations]? The lulls in business are tough to deal with. And then there are the prospective clients who are too wishy-washy about whether they want to hire you (especially during the lulls in business)." —**Adam Neufer (class of 2009)**

"[Frustrations]? I constantly wonder how to get more clients. I mean, where are they? Why do they go to Attorney X? How does Attorney X have such a huge caseload? It's sleep-depriving."
—**Kara O'Donnell (class of 1995)**

"It's frustrating to have clients who expect you to be available 24/7. I admit I didn't discourage that in the beginning, but now I'm better at managing my personal time. I schedule client phone calls just as if they were in-person meetings, unless it's a true emergency. That lets clients know that I value my time AND their time (no wasted phone-tag games)." —**Jan M. Tamanini (class of 1984)**

"Every day I start off thinking today is the day I am going to get caught up. But by the time I've finished breakfast at my desk, that illusion is gone because four people called, my receptionist is telling me a fifth is on the line, and there are four emails requiring immediate attention (and hundreds that can wait)!"
—**Lynda L. Hinkle (class of 2009)**

"Apart from those frustrations inherent in the legal system, my only frustrations have to do with [how I] prioritize and allocate my time. More often than I would like, I find myself cramming on some deadline because more immediate deadlines popped up and forced me to push work to the last minute." —**Mitchell J. Matorin (class of 1993)**

"What's always frustrating is making sure that invoices go out on a regular basis. That often takes away from completing projects and getting work done for clients."
—**Jeffrey G. Neu (class of 2006)**

"My main frustration is that there is so much to do and so little time to do it. When you have a skill-set that you believe will benefit potential clients, it is only natural to want to communicate that to potential clients. But getting face time with all of these potential clients is not always easy, and advertising is not always the best way to communicate your skills."
—**Kevin Afghani (class of 2004)**

"[What's often frustrating] is meeting a new opposing counsel, and [watching them] pause as they wonder if as a solo I might not be a very good lawyer. With practice, though, I'm starting to enjoy these moments."
—**Matthew G. Kaiser (class of 2002)**

"[If you haven't heard], solo practitioners are the red-headed stepchildren of the legal profession. And the consensus is that if we were really good lawyers, we'd be working for one big firm or another. My frustration is with this persistent, subtle hostility, especially when I hear that how I choose to practice law (collaborative family), how I choose to bill my clients (mostly fixed fees, a little hourly), and that I chose to solo right out of law school, is backwards, wrong, silly; perhaps even bordering on malpractice. The one bright spot is that, occasionally, I talk with a lawyer (usually a solo/small) who gets what I'm trying to do and why I'm trying to do it, and gives me heartfelt wishes for success. Beyond that, most of my daily frustrations are those any business experiences; clients who pay late and vendors who deliver late. But these are transient frustrations, and can be corrected with the proper administration of chocolate, riding my horses, and —in extreme cases —Scotch." **—Bruce Cameron (class of 2007)**

"My biggest frustration was, and still is, the realization that law school did nothing to prepare me for actual practice. I thought for sure that toiling those three years —under constant stress and anxiety —would provide the knowledge I needed to practice law. I am just amazed how precious little I learned about real-life litigation in law school, and that feeling has not waned. I almost admire those graduates who show up to court with improper filings and unfounded arguments because at least they're learning by trial and error." **—Gina Bongiovi (class of 2007)**

"[Mentors] play a huge role. So many answers aren't printed in books. You need [to find someone] to whom you can ask tons of stupid questions; someone you trust . . . and someone who respects what you're doing." **—Eric P. Ganci (class of 2008)**

"I cannot imagine starting a practice without a mentor and/or lawyer contacts to help. I always run things by other lawyers before I act." **—Marc W. Matheny (class of 1980)**

"Mentors and contacts are lifelines; when you need to figure out how this bit of law works . . . or how that form really needs to be formatted . . . or why sending one check to the county recorder will get your deed bounced back while sending two gets it recorded. Ask your mentor. Mentors and contacts are also your source for referrals (but it is also a two-way street; you have to give as well as receive.)" **—Bruce Cameron (class of 2007)**

"Mentors and contacts are invaluable; books and CLE's can take you only so far. A mentor can help you brainstorm ideas, guide you in making decisions, and keep you from falling on your face. Finding a mentor can be a challenge. But once a potential mentor walks into your life, show your appreciation and ask if you can lean on them for help. Most will find it flattering and a very rewarding way of giving back." **—Gina Bongiovi (class of 2007)**

"Mentors have been a huge part of my practice. Many times I come to a situation where I don't quite know the next step, or how to proceed in a case. After I have done as much research as I can, I will call a mentor or a colleague who practices in that area and bounce the idea off of them. I find that lawyers are almost always willing to talk out

a case or scenario with you. And when they call me for help, I always make sure I am available to repay the favor. If you get involved in bar associations and groups, you are bound to meet many people in the field who will be able to help you when you are stuck in a situation."
—**Paul Scott (class of 2008)**

"Having other attorneys for informal advice is an essential element of my practice. As a solo, you don't have the collegiality of other attorneys just down the hall to trade ideas and opinions—so you have to go to your bar groups or other formal and informal legal organizations to get that contact."
—**Jan M. Tamanini (class of 1984)**

"One of the things I commonly hear from other lawyers is that the best clients come from referrals, as opposed to mass marketing techniques. This is true in my case. So, I consider mentors and contacts to be very important in building your practice. [In fact], they are the only reason I've made money so far in my practice."
—**Kevin Afghani (class of 2004)**

How do you find, and work with, a mentor?

Mentors are key to succeeding, especially if you're a new lawyer. But even if you're a seasoned practitioner, a mentor can act as a Sherpa to guide you through the nitty-gritty issues related to starting and running a practice.

How to find and work with a mentor?

Start close and expand. To find a mentor, begin with solos you know. But don't limit yourself to personal acquaintances. Listservs and social media are a terrific resource for finding mentors outside your existing circle. As you spend time on a listserv or social media forums like LinkedIn or Twitter, you'll get to know other participants who share your background, and who offer particularly useful advice or who work nearby. Once you've identified someone with whom you'd like to work, set up a meeting or arrange a call to ask some questions. At the close of your meeting or talk, ask if you can follow up with other questions. Needless to say, follow up with a thank-you.

Don't be shy. Most solos give freely of their time, and are usually flattered when asked to help out a new solo.

Don't take advantage. The purpose of a mentor is to provide informal advice and feedback when you're out of your depth . . . not to serve as an unpaid consultant on a matter for which you're being well-compensated. Nor should you take the forms, pleadings, and knowledge that a mentor generously supplied and use the materials to poach your mentor's clients. Don't be a "foul-weather" mentee who contacts a mentor only when there's a problem. Keep in touch with your mentors every few months to let them know how you're doing even if you don't have a specific question. Want to know more about mentoring? Get a copy of *The Lawyer's Guide to Mentoring* by Ida Abbott, Esq.

20. What role do mentors play in your practice?

"I have online mentors at the listserv for the National Association of Consumer Bankruptcy Attorneys (NACBA), and I have a marketing mentor who plays a big role. But I wish I had a mentor for the substantive law. People are just too busy, though I'm still working on finding this."
—**Mark Tanney (class of 1998)**

"Find mentors; in fact, find more than one. In-person or online. And use your state bar resources. Most state bars have practice management advisers who will provide guidance for free. Also most state bars have numbers you can call to chat with an ethics counselor. If you are unsure about something you are doing, ask around and get more than one opinion on the subject. Then make your own informed decision. As a solo, no one else in the office is going to remind you to stay updated on your practice area. You've got to continue to stay updated and learn on your own so you have to be very self-motivated. If you don't have prior experience, realize that you will have to find ways to continue to learn and grow as a professional or your practice will stagnate with you."
—**Stephanie Kimbro (class of 2003)**

"I wish I had more [mentors], but so many other attorneys are too busy to mentor."
—**Kara O'Donnell (class of 1995)**

21. What role do people skills play in a solo's success?

"People skills are crucial. Most solos are the face of their firm in marketing efforts and must be accessible and approachable. No matter your practice area, you will do some amount of counseling and deal with people's emotions. Having the skills to manage your reactions and keep the client calm will serve you well."
—**Gina Bongiovi (class of 2007)**

"[People skills] are crucial. I occasionally meet other lawyers whose personalities leave something to be desired, and I know they would never make it as a solo. I feel like telling them they should thank their lucky stars they have the partners and paralegals to do it all for them."
—**Lynda L. Hinkle (class of 2009)**

"[People skills] are essential, unless you do transactional work and/or have a gregarious partner. In litigation, I have to get along okay with opposing counsel and well with my client(s). Getting along well with referral sources is obviously important, too." —**Michael Moebes (class of 2003)**

"People skills are essential. Law firms and corporate law departments can [employ] individuals who are skilled attorneys but not as good with people. But as a [solo] attorney, what I have to market is myself. And if I am unable to interact skillfully with people, it will be very difficult to build a client base. I think it would be very difficult to be successful as a solo without people skills." —**Cailie A. Currin (class of 1988)**

"I believe [people skills] are essential. People return to an attorney with whom they feel comfortable, and one they feel they can trust."
—**Abbe W. McClane (class of 2003)**

21. **What role do people skills play in a solo's success?**

"People skills are an absolute necessity. When I look at how much my personal interactions have increased since going solo, I don't see how it would be possible without being able to effectively interact with others. For someone trying to build a client base from the ground up, you will be interacting with others extensively. People skills should be developed or practiced."
—**Kevin Afghani (class of 2004)**

"People skills are among the most important. Managing relationships and expectations will determine if you are successful or not in a solo practice."—**Jeffrey G. Neu (class of 2006)**

"When you are a solo practitioner, you are the sole identity of your firm. The way you present yourself and deal with others has a direct impact on the image and success of your practice. Solo practitioners need to be able to effectively communicate with potential clients to generate business. You need to be able to handle clients to promote trust and cooperation. Sometimes interpersonal skills can make or break a case; other times, the manner in which you handle yourself in one matter can impact certain aspects of another matter. You do not have to be a 'people-person', but you must have good interpersonal and communication skills and have a sense of diplomacy and social tact."
—**Adam Neufer (class of 2009)**

"If you're in a business transactional practice, you can't emphasize your people skills enough. You simply won't get clients if you can't engage the people in your target pool."
—**Jan M. Tamanini (class of 1984)**

"[In a solo practice], the niche is in how you treat your clients, not in necessarily what area of law you practice."—**A Houston solo**

"An attorney's personality can be the difference between a potential client wanting to come in to sign up, and wanting to call a few other places. In general, clients like that I care about their problem, and take (a lot of) time to talk to them even on the first call."
—**Kara O'Donnell (class of 1995)**

"You have to have basic people skills. I'm far from a social butterfly or a marketing maven. But I like my clients and my clients like me, and I always go out of my way to be available, respectful, and informative. I think that's what clients really want most of the time. I'm proof that you don't need to be the type of person who becomes the focus of attention when he enters the room."
—**Mitchell J. Matorin (class of 1993)**

"People skills are important, but I don't think it is essential that you have a super outgoing personality. When you network, just ask people about themselves and pay attention; and when you work with clients, treat them with respect, keep your promises, and stay in touch. Those are the things that matter. If you are also really friendly and outgoing, that will be a plus . . . but not essential." —**Mark Tanney (class of 1998)**

"Good people skills are a must. You must make clients comfortable with you so that they retain you and send referrals to you, and you must make colleagues and others believe in your practice so that they give the assistance you need or send referrals."—**Tonya Coles (class of 2006)**

"Those lawyers who present themselves in a competent and professional fashion are likely to be able to get behind what the client is saying, and really understand what they need. Part of [a lawyer's] skill-set is the ability to hear the [client's] words, but to also understand and appreciate the hidden meaning. Clients don't always share the details and you have to pry it out of them before taking action." —**Bruce L. Dorner (class of 1977)**

"I do mostly immigration law, deportation defense, and criminal defense. People skills have been extremely important in my business. And as a relatively new attorney, I made sure to offer extremely good customer service so that client's would feel comfortable with me, and be more inclined to hire me." —**Paul Scott (class of 2008)**

"If you can treat people with simple courtesy and respect when you are having a bad day, you have sufficient people skills to be a successful solo. I have no doubt that the better your people skills, the easier it will be being a solo" —**Bruce Cameron (class of 2007)**

PART THREE:
The Business of Solo'ing

22. What business skills are essential for a solo?

23. How do you market your legal practice?

24. What marketing advice do you have for
    new solos?

25. What financial issues loom in a solo's first year?

26. Can you solo on a shoestring budget?

27. What about job security?

28. How important is a business plan?

29. What would you tell new solos about
    malpractice insurance?

30. What role does social media play in marketing
    your practice and building relationships?

31. What are you doing to stay profitable?

32. What is your Plan B if things don't work out?

Inroduction

Inroduction

22. What business skills are essential for a solo?

Many lawyers, myself included, chafe at the notion that law is a business. After all, many of us chose to become lawyers to join a noble profession: to solve clients' problems; to defend the innocent; to vindicate constitutional principles; to fight for justice. We see ourselves as professionals not used car salesman. Still, like it or not, solos have no choice but to accept and master the business aspects of starting and running a law firm.

As a solo, you may want to take every First Amendment case that walks in the door, but if the clients can't pay you'll have to close the doors. You can choose to ignore or outsource such mundane tasks as bookkeeping or safeguarding files. But sooner or later, you'll face a grievance if a client asks for a document that you can't locate, or if the bar discovers that your trust accounts aren't properly reconciled. And while you may prefer to sit back and wait for the phone to ring instead of doing something as undignified as marketing, you will likely wind up with the rejects that dozens of other lawyers spurned before they came to you.

In short, the only way you can succeed in the legal profession is to focus on the business aspects that will keep your firm afloat. Here's how others solos are doing it . . . in their own words.

"QuickBooks."—**Lynda L. Hinkle (class of 2009)**

"You must know or understand your firm's financials. If you don't understand them, get a CPA or an accountant who can keep you on track."—**Gina Bongiovi (class of 2007)**

"Unless you're planning to hire a CPA, you should at least gain some basic knowledge in federal income tax to ensure that you are not over- or under- paying your taxes. I was pretty freaked out to learn that I was required to pay a quarterly estimated tax to the IRS based on my projected income, and that my failure to pay this quarterly estimated tax could result in an underpayment penalty."—**Kevin Afghani (class of 2004)**

"The use of accounting/billing software was the hardest for me, and I definitely floundered in trying to get that financial part of the practice established correctly. I felt lucky to have clients to bill, but I was not very proficient in getting those first few bills out. I spent a lot of money on an accountant to do it right after I had tried on my own."—**Cailie A. Currin (class of 1988)**

"Solos need to learn that running a law office is a business, with budgets, costs, potential overruns, unexpected crises, etc."—**Marc W. Matheny (class of 1980)**

"Budgeting, time management, and marketing. These are smart business practices, and ignoring them can mean your solo practice won't survive. Also, you must know the difference between doing a good job for your clients and overkill. Spending too much time and effort on simple matters because you're a perfectionist—or you want to win —is counterproductive for both you and your clients. Knowing how to negotiate and

64 PART THREE: The Business of Solo'ing

22. What business skills are essential for a solo?

compromise while getting a good deal for your client is something you can learn over time, but many attorneys never bother."
—**Jan M. Tamanini (class of 1984)**

"From a business point of view, the bare minimum skill-set would be: can you balance a checkbook, do you have the discipline to balance your accounts every month, can you write up an invoice, can you send out bills, and do you know when to talk to an accountant? As for the legal skill-set, that depends on what type of law you are going to practice. At a minimum: know how to do legal research without using Lexis or Westlaw, where the nearest law library is, how to read and evaluate a contract, how to do a conflicts check, how to get an ethics question answered, how to find statutes, how to get your CLE credits recorded, how to record a deed, draft a complaint, how to get something served, where the courthouse is, where the courtrooms are, what preliminary information you need to evaluate a matter, how to talk to a client, and who the court clerks are." —**Bruce Cameron (class of 2007)**

"As a solo practitioner you are responsible for every aspect of the practice. Businesswise, you need to learn how to do pretty much everything. As to legal skills, law school does not teach you how to be a lawyer; it teaches you how conduct legal research and writing. You need to learn how to be a lawyer as well."
—**Adam Neufer (class of 2009)**

"The most important skill is in knowing when to say 'no' to a potential client."
—**Bruce L. Dorner (class of 1977)**

23. How do you market your legal practice?

"I've tried advertising twice, and it hasn't worked at all. I network [now], almost exclusively"
—**Gina Bongiovi (class of 2007)**

"I use a variety of [marketing methods]: blogging, social networks, and I'm active in my local bar organizations and the ABA."
—**Jeffrey G. Neu (class of 2006)**

"My blog works well. And I send letters [to clients] on a regular basis. It works wonders."
—**Thomas J. Crane (class of 1983)**

"I have a blog on insurance coverage issues . . . I have a tagline on my emails and listserv comments that lets people know what I do . . . and I make cold calls to attorneys. All these have worked well." —**Nina Kallen (class of 1994)**

"Blogging, Web sites, Twitter, Facebook. They all have worked very well. Joining organizations (e.g., GTLA, AAJ, STLA, etc.) has been good for meeting attorneys to whom I can send work (and from whom I can receive work)."
—**Michael Moebes (class of 2003)**

"I have found that online marketing works for me, and that print advertising does not work for me. My online advertising is targeted to my areas of practice, and the calls I get based on these usually result in business. The calls I get from print advertising, on the other hand, seems to be from people seeking a legal service that I don't offer." —**Tonya Coles (class of 2006)**

"I market myself in the area where I enjoy practicing: real estate, probate, elder law, using written advertising, TV, and networking with others in the same venues."
—**Abbe W. McClane (class of 2003)**

"Most of my marketing is in-person contact at networking events, committees, and the like. I have received an increasing amount of referrals through word-of-mouth. I hired a friend to design my Web site and I also use social media such as Twitter, LinkedIn, and Facebook. I've even had a small amount of luck on Craigslist."
—**Jenny Jeltes (class of 2006)**

"[What works for me] is a Web site that seems to attract clients. I also write a fair amount for several publications and online outlets. I answer questions on Avvo in my practice areas and my location. I network in local business, alumni, and community groups. And I tout where I'm different from most attorneys (I don't bill hourly except in certain exceptional situations, and I emphasize plain English in my documents). All of it adds up. I haven't spent much on print advertising, because I don't think it's effective for attorneys who don't do personal injury or family law."
—**Jan M. Tamanini (class of 1984)**

"My first efforts at marketing—a Web site and a small Yellow Pages ad —were aimed at increasing my firm's visibility to the public and potential clients. I got little response. So, I decided to increase my firm's visibility within the legal community, and sent a mass e-mail to former law school classmates and to legal employers. The response was immediate! I received a few client referrals within the first month of launching my firm. Now, I have turned my attention to promoting my firm and networking with non-legal professionals whose services overlap with my own. I believe that it is not who you know, but who knows you that makes the difference."
—**Adam Neufer (class of 2009)**

"One big marketing don't concerns phone directory advertising. If you can't afford to put a full page ad on the cover, or in the front of the attorney's section, don't bother spending money on anything other than the minimal listing. Phone directories are for finding business that you already know exist, not for discovering new businesses. I've also had a poor ROI from social networking and on-line referral services like Avvo and Martindale. They were all very expensive in actual dollars or the investment in time. What works? Networking and referrals (note: happy clients are repeat clients, and happy clients refer new clients). And for some reason imprinted pens have been an effective form of marketing. I have pens imprinted with the name of my law firm and a contact number, and leave them in check-out lanes, at gas stations, on restaurant tables, and with anyone patting their pockets. Once free from my control, those pens occasionally wind up in the hands of someone who wants a lawyer."
—**Bruce Cameron (class of 2007)**

"Face-to-face meetings are most important. A solo needs to get out to bar meetings, Chamber of Commerce events, club events, and alumni meetings, to let others know what they are doing."
—**Brian M. Annino (class of 2003)**

"I think involvement in the local and state bar associations is very helpful, because it gets your name out among other lawyers. For years, I also put an ad in our church bulletin. I got an awful lot of clients that way, and the cost was minimal."
—**Marc W. Matheny (class of 1980)**

"One thing I can say does not work is to network with people who are unlikely to have legal work [in your practice area], or who are unlikely to know someone who needs legal work. As a patent attorney, I would consider it unwise to join an organization consisting primarily of realtors and insurance agents. These professions have little or no exposure to intellectual property, and are therefore unlikely to know anyone needing patent services." —**Kevin Afghani (class of 2004)**

"I've participated in many pro bono or 'low bono' events. Not only have I helped good causes, but I met many people who eventually referred business to me because of my involvement. I think that is an excellent way to get your name out there and to enjoy your work at the same time."
—**Paul Scott (class of 2008)**

"[In marketing], there is nothing better than satisfied clients who refer business to your office. The next best source is other attorneys who have conflicts, are too busy, or whose case may be too small for them. Also, never steal a client! Always send the client back to the referring attorney. If the client won't go back, make sure the referring attorney knows from the client that it was their decision, not yours."
—**Bruce L. Dorner (class of 1977)**

"Don't be afraid to refer cases to other attorneys, and to volunteer your time either inside or outside the legal field." —**Eric P. Ganci (class of 2008)**

"I've had a full-time marketing staff member for about a year, and so far I'm thrilled with the arrangement. The quality of my materials and the amount of name recognition I have in my field has increased tremendously."
—**Cailie A. Currin (class of 1988)**

"Get your name out there. Start a Web site, teach a class, volunteer at the bar association."
—**Marc W. Matheny (class of 1980)**

"Spend at least 50 percent of your time marketing . . . and don't just rely on the Internet. Go out and meet people; shake hands; hand out cards; go to networking events; go to charity events. Make sure every person you meet knows what you do and how to reach you."
—**Lynda L. Hinkle (class of 2009)**

"Marketing should be one of the most important goals in the beginning of your practice . . . and throughout. Because if you don't market yourself, it doesn't matter how great an attorney you are. And if you stop marketing when it's busy, and only market when it's slow, your message and presence will not be consistent and clients will smell your desperation." —**Gabriel Cheong (class of 2007)**

"My advice is spend most of your time marketing . . . especially at the beginning. You may be able to spend less time later, but marketing will always be a major part of your practice. And even though it may not come naturally to you, you need to make an effort to continue. There are many ways to market oneself online: blogging, social media, e-mail marketing, search engine optimization. Learn everything you can about this, and put a lot of effort into it. And find ways to network in the real world . . . but in a way that makes sense for you. Don't just attend Chamber of Commerce meetings and hand out your business card to 100 people (although that may not make sense if you are a criminal defense attorney). Find the networking methods that make sense for your practice area and do those."
—**Mark Tanney (class of 1998)**

"The best marketing by far is word-of-mouth. Always do a good job, you will be surprised how many people are paying attention."
—**Jenee Oliver (class of 2005)**

"Never underestimate the power of face-to-face networking." —**Brian M. Annino (class of 2003)**

"Have a good elevator speech and use it. And specialize. Other attorneys will remember you if you are really good at one thing, and will refer clients to you."—**Nina Kallen (class of 1994)**

"As a new solo, it is more important to market yourself to other attorneys and professionals than to market yourself to the general public. Having a Web site and Yellow Pages ad is good, but don't expect much response from them in the beginning." —**Adam Neufer (class of 2009)**

"Network with other attorneys. Go out of your way to be helpful, and to go beyond the expected when somebody asks for advice. Join the ABA's Solosez listserv and actively participate and show your experience and willingness to help. And always be available for brainstorming with other attorneys. Get a good Web site; it doesn't have to be expensive, but it does have to be professional, informative, and most of all, it has to exist."
—**Mitchell J. Matorin (class of 1993)**

"Network, network, network. For some reason, I always discounted how important it was, probably because I am an introvert. I finally started networking with financial planners and other attorneys and it has been invaluable."
—**Sarah White (class of 2002)**

"Put yourself out there. Join networking and community groups, and ask your friends if they know anyone to whom they could send your name as a referral. Don't be afraid to ask clients or networking colleagues to pass your name along to their friends, customers, and business partners, and don't get discouraged if someone doesn't hire you immediately. It might take months, it might take years. And have your elevator pitch ready and tailored to the group you're with at the time. Write articles for your bar publications; write op-ed pieces for local papers and magazines on general interest issues in your area of expertise . . . and ALWAYS carry business cards with you. You never know when you might run into someone who could use your help, or who may know someone else who does." —**Jan M. Tamanini (class of 1984)**

"Keep meeting people, even if it doesn't appear to be getting any [immediate] results. And keep in mind, there is a ton of ways to market yourself; do one that you're going to stick with and be comfortable with for the long haul. You didn't solo to become someone else's clone, so don't copy a marketing plan with which you are not comfortable."—**Matthew G. Kaiser (class of 2002)**

"Advertising is usually a waste of money unless you have a war chest to throw at a campaign designed to put your name in front of people at least seven times. Instead, I have found networking to be the most profitable. Not just any networking, though. I spun my wheels in networking groups for about six months, signing very few clients because I was marketing to the wrong audience . . . potential clients. Now, I network and market to my referral sources, and it has made all the difference. Over the past two years, I've honed my group of referral sources to maybe a dozen different people, and now I work on building those relationships. To find your own referral sources, think of other people who come into contact with your same target client. For example, if you do estate planning, who else might deal with that type of client—bankers, financial planners, CPAs, family lawyers, real estate agents, etc? Regardless of your practice area, work on building relationships with your referral sources and they will do the selling for you." —**Gina Bongiovi (class of 2007)**

"I'm a fairly recent solo [still] learning myself. But identifying your ideal type of client, and then finding a way to make a connection with that type of client will ensure that you're spending your time in activities most likely to be effective. If you have a specialty, [ask yourself whether] that specialty is to your advantage by narrowing your potential client field, and then persistently pursue clients in this narrowed field. As a patent attorney, my goal is to know as many technology decision-makers as possible; these are the type of people most likely to need and acquire my patent counsel."
—**Kevin Afghani (class of 2004)**

"I recommend that solos add to their monthly to-do list the task of staying updated on technology, especially social media applications and forms of online networking. Since this is how our clients are searching for, and reviewing us as lawyers, we need to be out there building our online presence and brand to stay competitive. Also, don't overthink your online marketing. Yes, comply with the rules of professional conduct. But that doesn't mean your online presence has to be antiseptic or robotic. Be human online, and don't relate to clients and fellow attorneys with a slew of disclaimers and warnings."
—**Stephanie Kimbro (class of 2003)**

"From the books I read, I distilled a common thread: even if I did not do a formal marketing plan, I should start with a clear vision of what I wanted my practice to be, and then make all my decisions to be consistent with that vision."
—**Dean N. Alterman (class of 1989)**

"Know your audience. Think about your ideal client, and about what that client's needs are and where that client can be found. Then, find the most effective—and least expensive—methods for marketing to that type of client. Start a Facebook page and a Twitter account, and update them regularly with information relevant to the audience you are trying to attract. Also, pay a professional to build the best Web site you can afford. Your site is the face of your practice and should be built to put your best image forward."
—**Tonya Coles (class of 2006)**

"The more you know about your ideal client, and the more detailed description you have of that ideal client, the more cost-effective your marketing will be. Three suggestions:
a) Tailor your marketing to your ideal client, and don't waste time, effort or money on marketing methods that will not reach that ideal client. If your ideal client is between 60 and 80 years of age, male, living on a farm, you may not want to spend a great deal of time building up your social media contacts or your web site's SEO because your client is not likely to see them. But if your ideal client is age 25-35, an urban professional working in software design, your online presence will be vitally important.
b) When preparing marketing materials, you must get across who you are, what you offer, why you should be hired, where you are located, and how to contact you in an efficient manner.

c) Have a uniform look across all your materials (same colors, same type faces, etc.), and a consistent presence. If you take an ad out in the local shopper, keep it going for several weeks, even months. Name recognition takes time and patience."
—**Bruce Cameron (class of 2007)**

"Before starting my firm, I went to a seminar on going solo. One of the presenters—a very successful personal injury lawyer—offered a piece of marketing advice that I will never forget: 'the best marketing you can do is to respect your clients, because even a client with a small personal injury case might have a cousin, a brother, a friend, etc., who may one day have a million dollar case . . . and you want to make sure you get that referral.' This stuck with me, and is something I use in my practice today. My advice [to new solos] is to be a people person and give EVERYONE respect. I have gotten more clients from just being present at events and being nice to people. I have given free consultations to people who did not retain me because there was nothing I could do to help them, or because they could not afford the fee. They should still be treated like they are the most important person in the office and don't forget to give them some (many) cards on the way out! They will usually take them gladly, and they will be your biggest referral sources before you know it." —**Paul Scott (class of 2008)**

"Join civil, social and fraternal organizations, and shake hands with as many people as you can."
—**Brian Rabal (class of 2005)**

"Cultivate relationships. At least once a week, I have lunch (or coffee) with a colleague, a former client, or a potential referral source. I track personal and professional information for everyone I come into contact with, so that if I run across something that might be helpful or of interest I can forward it to them. And volunteering to chair the employment law section of my state's trial lawyer association has been a wonderful opportunity to meet more experienced employment law attorneys and to raise my profile." —**D. Jill Pugh (class of 1994)**

"Make friends with lawyers in all practice areas. If you take them out and give them a nice lunch —even attorneys making $200, $300 an hour —will be willing to chat about your legal work from time to time. Think of it as an investment. You want to get on their radar, so they take your phone calls, answer your questions, and refer you work. Also, make thank-you calls and send thank-you notes. During the holidays, I send Starbucks gift cards. What lawyer doesn't love coffee?"
—**Sergio Benavides (class of 2005)**

"Getting good clients is all about networks; hometown, college, law school, government, firm, etc. Unless you have two or three good, separate networks, making it as a solo is very difficult. Which means that unless you spend a lot on advertising, you may have to spend a decade or more building up your networks before going out on your own." —**Mark Del Bianco (class of 1980)**

"Keep marketing, and never ever rest on your laurels." —**Walter D. James III (class of 1987)**

24. What marketing advice do you have for new solos?

"The best marketing I've ever done has been to write articles for a publication read by my target clients. It's free publicity, and I always get calls. I suggest that solos find those publications (relevant to their practice) and get published. It's free marketing . . . and it works."
—**Traci D. Ellis (class of 1990)**

"My advice is to read business and marketing books. Not just the books for attorneys (although those are also helpful), but the general business advertising books. Second, billboard ads will not make you rich, and direct mail and Yellow Pages ads do little good. Advertising only works when many mediums are combined, and the message is consistent. The only way ads will be remembered is if they are everywhere."
—**Scott Wolfe (class of 2005)**

25. What financial issues loom in a solo's first year?

"Cash flow is the biggest [issue]. A solo starting with few clients (say, enough to keep him or her busy only about half time) will have to watch expenses carefully and wait for the practice to grow." —**Dean N. Alterman (class of 1989)**

"I think the biggest [financial issue] is cash flow. In order to effectively practice, you need to be able to bridge the gap between billing and receiving." —**Cailie A. Currin (class of 1988)**

"Overhead and cash flow. Those are the biggest financial issues that can sink a solo at any time." —**Herb Dubin (class of 1964)**

"Expect cash flow to be a major concern for at least the first two years of your practice. In the majority of cases, it takes substantial time to build up a client base, and therefore it might be necessary to do other work to pay the bills."
—**Jenny Jeltes (class of 2006)**

"Your first year of soloing is all about budgeting. You saved up or borrowed just enough money to get you through the first year. The challenge is figuring out what to spend your money on and what to skimp on. Office space, a landline phone, and a secretary are not that necessary in the first year." —**Gabriel Cheong (class of 2007)**

"The biggest financial issue that looms the first year is not having income. After that first year you will probably have built enough receivables to weather a dry spell. But, basically, that first year will likely be a dry spell with little receivables and savings."
—**Paul Scott (class of 2008)**

"[Financial issue]? Debt avoidance. Contingency-fee practices take time to pay out. And self-employment taxes suck. I way underestimated my tax liability in Year 1."
—**Michael Moebes (class of 2003)**

"Building a solo practice requires a good amount of start-up capital. It takes time to start producing income and even more time to start producing a profit. One of the biggest financial issues in going solo is deciding how to set your fees. I needed to be extremely creative with billing in my first year of solo-ing. For certain cases I set an hourly fee, and for others I offered a fixed-rate fee. A lot of the time I offered discounted rates."
—**Adam Neufer (class of 2009)**

"Don't put your practice on a credit card or borrow from friends/relatives. Who needs that stress?"
—**Eric P. Ganci (class of 2008)**

"Try to have a savings account or line of credit until you're at least breaking even."
—**Abbe W. McClane (class of 2003)**

"You will [have to] budget for malpractice insurance, office equipment, law books, training materials, and seminars. And you will need to join your state bar association, and probably additional local associations as well. Everything will be more expensive than you expect it to be. Even networking. Between transportation to and from the location, and then buying a drink or a sandwich, it can easily cost you $25 to attend an event. That can add up to hundreds a month if you are an active networker (which you need to be). You need to think about all this."
—**Mark Tanney (class of 1998)**

"Malpractice insurance, health insurance, student loans . . . and [making sure to] to pay yourself."
—**Lynda L. Hinkle (class of 2009)**

"Malpractice insurance; that's a couple of thousand right out of the gate. [As far as overhead was concerned] I kept it down by working out of my house. With a transactional practice, I didn't need a lot of space to meet clients."
—**Jeffrey G. Neu (class of 2006)**

"At a minimum, you need to budget for a laptop, a scanner, a laser printer, business cards, and a back-up system for your laptop (and, yes, you do need a backup system; preferably two. One that stores backups off-site and one that stores locally). And malpractice insurance. Talk with the insurance agent about how to minimize your premium. Maybe investing in practice management software can reduce your premium, or emphasizing one practice area over another may change your level of risk and thus lower your premium. You'll also need an accountant at least three times during your first year: to set up your books and learn how to maintain them, to start planning for the year's taxes, and again at tax time. If you solo right out of law school, you need to consider how to make your student loan payments. Talk with your loan servicer to see if you qualify for a deferment or a reduced payment plan. It's easier to work with lenders before there are problems." —**Bruce Cameron (class of 2007)**

"Pick and choose carefully where your money will go. Don't go nuts and buy everything you think you might want. For example, don't buy a lot of books. You won't use many of them very much, and a lot of the time they're available at one of your local law libraries."
—**Jan M. Tamanini (class of 1984)**

How much should I charge?

Every discussion about legal fees ultimately returns to one of two questions: how much should I charge, and how do I make sure to get paid? This is true whether it's a debate over the billable hour versus alternative-fee structure . . . the wisdom of competing for clients on price . . . whether to charge for an initial consultation . . . the level of detail you should include on your bills . . . or whether to sue a client to collect an unpaid bill. Most lawyers make the mistake of addressing these two questions independently without realizing their interrelationship. Ultimately, your firm's profitability hinges on how you resolve both of these issues.

Consider three examples:

John Smith decides to charge clients $2,500 (five times the going rate) to prepare a simple will, theorizing that a well-drafted will saves money by minimizing the possibility of an expensive and protracted will contest by a disgruntled heir. Though reasonable in theory, Smith is unlikely to find clients who can have their pick of lawyers who provide the same service at a fraction of the price. Bottom line: Smith has given thought to how much he should charge, but ignored the question of how he can ensure that he gets paid.

Jane Short is retained to represent a client in a possible age-discrimination action. She explains to the client that she bills $200/hour, and requires a $10,000 retainer to cover her first 50 hours of work. Without inquiring about the client's budget, Ms. Short recommends and embarks on an aggressive litigation strategy. Even before discovery has concluded, she exhausts the retainer, and puts in an additional $10,000 worth of time for which she has not been compensated. When she bills the client for unpaid fees, and asks the client to replenish the retainer amount, the client says she's out of money. Bottom line: Jane knew how much to charge, but she gave no thought to whether her strategy fit her client's budget, and how to get paid if it didn't.

Ralph Young, just a few weeks after starting his practice, receives a referral to represent a large apartment complex in eviction proceedings. The landlord agrees to pay Ralph $1,500/month to appear in landlord-tenant court four days a month. Each court appearance would last no more than three hours, for a total of 12 hours per month or a rate of $125/hour (not bad for a new attorney). Like clockwork, the landlord pays Young his fee at the beginning of each month. After a few months, Young's practice picks up and he finds that he's working late at the office to compensate for the time spent in landlord-tenant court. Moreover, with the half-hour of prep required for each appearance . . . and the hour-long commute to and from court . . . he's spending closer to 18 hours a month on the matter, reducing his fee to $83/hour. Bottom line: Young has no problem getting paid. But he neglected to take to calculate the true cost of his time, i.e., what to charge for the arrangement.

25. What financial issues loom in a solo's first year?

"All your necessary equipment needs to be purchased in the beginning; computer, a backup storage device, a printer, scanner, copier, basic office supplies, and a Dictaphone if you dictate. You also need to decide if you want to lease space away from home. Personally, I worked out of my home for the first few months, and then found a modest space when my fiancé and I decided to move in together. For my patent practice, glamorous office space is not necessary, as I usually meet with my clients at their offices. You may also need to spend money on joining any desired organizations (e.g., bar associations, chambers of commerce)."
—**Kevin Afghani (class of 2004)**

"[When I started my firm], I didn't have much in the way of savings, and I financed my practice by drawing on my home equity line of credit. We lived frugally for a few months; not nearly as frugally as we could have or should have, but frugally enough. With the right technology and a home office, there's no reason why your overhead should be overwhelming."
—**Mitchell J. Matorin (class of 1993)**

26. Can you solo on a shoestring budget?

"Solo on a shoestring? Hell, yes. It's what I do every day! There are times when the money is coming in gangbusters, and other times when I wonder when I'll get new work to pay the bills. This unpredictability takes a strong stomach. But if you can get by without an ostentatious office and use the Internet and local resources to make your practice work, you really don't need to lay out the big bucks." —**Jan M. Tamanini (class of 1984)**

"Yes, you can solo on a shoestring. I meet clients at a mini-mart gas station/restaurant, and nobody has ever complained . . . especially when they get a free cappuccino and donut. For business clients, I make house calls . . . my office phone is ported to my cell phone . . . my desk and files are in a corner bedroom of my home . . . and some of my files and motion forms are in the back seat of my car. I run from courthouse to courthouse, and it's a blast; I never know what to expect. I like the drama and excitement, and being home by 1:30 or stopping at Borders every afternoon after court."
—**Anonymous**

"You can absolutely solo on a shoestring. With some splurges here and there, I spent $8,000 on my firm in the first seven months. My splurges? Hiring a graphic designer to do my logo, business cards and Web site; having separate business lines installed in my house; buying a new computer and printer. There is no reason that a brand new solo needs the fancy office, the secretary, the paralegal, the new car, the mahogany desk, and all those BigLaw trappings. In fact, many clients have said they chose a solo because we're perceived to be more agile, more streamlined, and less taken with pretentious surroundings that are simply reflected in the client's bill." —**Gina Bongiovi (class of 2007)**

"[Start on a shoestring]? Sure you can. You do not have to have extravagant furnishings. It depends on the area of practice, I suppose. But 'nice' was always good enough for my clients."
—**Thomas J. Crane (class of 1983)**

"Of course you can solo on a shoestring. You can practice from a home office or shared office, and you do not need a large, full time staff. I have practiced for 30 years and make a comfortable living without ever having had a full-time employee." —**Marc W. Matheny (class of 1980)**

"It depends on how you define shoestring. There are some things you can't skimp on: a basic office set-up, supplies, malpractice insurance, an accountant (at least at tax time), and money for networking/marketing events. Things you can skimp on: an expensive office and an assistant or paralegal to start out."
—**Lynda L. Hinkle (class of 2009)**

"[Start on a shoestring]? Definitely. My only real fixed costs are bar dues, CLE, and malpractice insurance. I work from home and make house calls or meet my clients somewhere in public. I was afraid I would appear unprofessional, but no one yet has questioned my professionalism because I don't meet them in my office. Instead, they seem thrilled that I come to them." —**Sarah White (class of 2002)**

"It depends on your practice. I opened with just a computer and an Internet connection. Now I have three attorneys who work for me."—**Jeffrey G. Neu (class of 2006)**

"I made it happen [solo'd] with about six months of expenses saved up. Now, with inexpensive technology, I think it's even more possible to begin on a shoestring. Of course, it helped that in my first year I was able to keep my overhead to $1,000/month." —**Michael Moebes (class of 2003)**

"In my practice area (patent preparation and prosecution), there is very little overhead and my equipment requirements are minimal. Whether you can solo on a shoestring or not depends on your practice area and your comfort level. Having more than a shoestring budget will allow you to persevere through periods with little or no income. But you wouldn't want to have to close your practice simply because you couldn't collect any fees for two or three months."
—**Kevin Afghani (class of 2004)**

"The cost to get up and running varies by region and practice setting. I know attorneys who work from their kitchen table and make a good living; I know others with beautiful offices and high overhead who barely break even. If you need the trappings to feel good and be productive, then the office setting is necessary. [But] clients generally don't like to pay for leather chairs and original artwork; they just want to see a clean, well-presented setting when they meet with you."—**Bruce L. Dorner (class of 1977)**

"You can set up a solo office on a shoestring; you just can't run a solo practice on one. All those articles on the '$10,000 law practice', the '$5,000 law office', and 'starting-a-law-practice-a-shoestring' are correct as far as they go. Their flaw? They don't consider what it costs to live AND maintain your practice. [As you prepare to solo], remember you need to factor in rent or mortgage payments, and those pesky bills for food, utilities, telephone, transportation, health insurance, and taxes. Then there are costs for professional marketing, maintaining your license,

and advancing court costs or filing fees on your client's behalf. On top of THOSE, there are the unexpected costs like the $500 brake job or the thousand-dollar medical bill. When I calculated my first-year expenses, estimates showed that my all-in costs would be $50,000-$75,000. These are big, scary, serious numbers. But better to go in prepared — and have a well considered budget — than to find out four months into your practice that you must decide between spending $500 on your mortgage or your office rent, or sending it to the district court because you have to cover the filing fees for that last-minute counter-complaint."
—**Bruce Cameron (class of 2007)**

"The number one reason new businesses fail is undercapitalization. I think most lawyers start off their firms on a shoestring, which makes a business plan even more important. [Before you solo], there should be a definite plan that lays out expenses and a few definite referral sources in place. The less money you have to start, the stricter your budget needs to be."
—**Paul Scott (class of 2008)**

"Who has job security? I think I have more than most. At least I know I won't fire myself!"
—**Lynda L. Hinkle (class of 2009)**

"I suppose it's no different than anyone else; none of us can count on our jobs. At least I know my boss won't fire me!"
—**Abbe W. McClane (class of 2003)**

"I have the greatest job security of almost any lawyer I know. The only person who can fire me is me. Right now, my biggest fear is NOT about job security, but whether I should to hire an associate to take some of my load because I have so much work." —**Marc W. Matheny (class of 1980)**

"The best part [of being solo] is that I cannot be fired. I've been caught up in those office politics things and [solo'ing] is much better. My success depends on no one but me."
—**Thomas J. Crane (class of 1983)**

"Job security at a law firm is a misnomer nowadays. [In fact], I have more job security now than I ever did working for a firm. At least now, I determine if and when I work, provided I have enough clients." —**Jeffrey G. Neu (class of 2006)**

"I guess it depends on your definition of 'job security'. From my perspective, I have the most secure job in the world. I can't be fired. I can lose a client, but I'll always be able to find others. I have no psychotic boss who enjoys making me feel as if I'm about to go in front of the firing squad every day. I know I have the skills and personality needed to succeed [as a solo]. To me that's more valuable than any salary."
—**Jan M. Tamanini (class of 1984)**

"As odd as this may sound, going solo can actually increase your job security by diversifying the sources from which you derive income. Conversely, when you work for a law firm, you derive income from a single source. Being in a firm can lull you into a false sense of security simply because you're receiving a paycheck at regular intervals. But what happens if you piss off one of the partners . . . or one of your superior partners loses a major client . . . or your firm is forced to lay off associates? Your single source of income suddenly becomes a past source of income, and you are left unemployed. From a certain perspective, going solo can actually be less risky than being an employee at a law firm." —**Kevin Afghani (class of 2004)**

"My colleagues at large firms may do work for many clients, but they have only one employer. [On the other hand], I have several dozen recurring clients (who I think of as my employers). [For this reason] I have much more job security than most of my colleagues at large firms."
—**Dean N. Alterman (class of 1989)**

"I do have job security. There's something secure in being your own boss and employing yourself. It's financial security that is my concern."
—**Ubong Akpan (class of 2003)**

"I kind of like [a lack of job security]. It makes life seem a lot more real, and it forces me to focus a little more on each day."
—**Matthew G. Kaiser (class of 2002)**

"[The lack of job security is scary]. It definitely keeps you working for business!"
—**Eric P. Ganci (class of 2008)**

"We create our own job security by finding clients and satisfying their needs. I actually feel greater job security in my practice now than in law firm life." —**Brian M. Annino (class of 2003)**

"It's definitely nerve-racking to go a few weeks without new or prospective business. But I would rather deal with that than the [uncertainty] that comes while waiting to hear whether you'll be laid off. I like it that my job security is more or less up to me." —**Adam Neufer (class of 2009)**

"I've learned to be OK with [a lack of job security]. In reality, you don't have much job security in a law firm anyway, as the last few years have demonstrated quite nicely. My job security now lies in my ability to get the job done, to have clients who think highly of me, and to respect what I've done for them."
—**Mitchell J. Matorin (class of 1993)**

"When I was trying to decide if I should solo, the thought of having little to no job security scared the willies out of me and made for sleepless nights. Now that I'm a solo, I come home so exhausted that sleeping is not a problem. Seriously, the lack of job security is worrisome, but that's just one of the trade-offs you make. It's all how you approach it; either you fret and worry about [the lack of job security], or it becomes the impetus to start marketing and building your practice." —**Bruce Cameron (class of 2007)**

"I believe in my own abilities and work ethic, and I think I have more job security working for myself. When I worked for a firm and in-house, there was always a certain amount of work that would just arrive and had to be done. Now [as a solo], I have to work hard and do a good job to make the work appear. As long as I continue to do that, I should be able to make a living and support my staff's livelihood." —**Cailie A. Currin (class of 1988)**

"When I put in my last two weeks at my former law firm, I was paralyzed by nervousness about going out on my own. It lasted all of two days. Then one day I just snapped out of it and realized that the only job security out there is the job security I create for myself. Once I started working in my own office I actually felt a sense of empowerment that I was creating my own job, and that no one was going to be able to take it away from me."
—**Paul Scott (class of 2008)**

"For better or worse, I have never really had job security so I don't really miss it. I worked as an independent contractor throughout college and law school, and jobs came sporadically. I suppose that's helped my frame of mind. In fact, I see friends who worked as loyal employees for over a decade [and who were] laid off with an hour's notice. No one these days has any job security. I might go so far as to argue the highest degree of job security is enjoyed by the self-employed."
—**Gina Bongiovi (class of 2007)**

"I think [solo practice] would be scary if I wasn't married with my spouse's support. However, from what I've seen, most lawyers (or most professions for that matter) don't have a ton of job security in today's market. In addition, I have seen my income steadily increase, which provides me with a feeling of security." —**Sarah White (class of 2002)**

"We seem to be moving away from the traditional BigLaw model. [In my opinion], working for a firm will provide little real job security as this trend continues. As a solo, I can never be fired and I can't be forced to retire. If I can get [my solo practice] off the ground, my job security will actually be greater."
—**Mark Tanney (class of 1998)**

"[A business plan] is extremely important. It provides you with a solid goal and a plan on how to achieve it. And then it projects past the goal to a greater one."
—**Abbe W. McClane (class of 2003)**

"A business plan is critical because it forces you to think about the type of practice you hope to establish, and it gives you insight into challenges and competetion. With a business plan, you will feel that you are better able to make informed decisions about your practice."
—**Tonya Coles (class of 2006)**

"Business plans are important, but they don't have to be 50 pages long. [Mine was] a mission-and-vision statement, with a budget, some goals, and the names of everyone I would contact about referrals. That was about it."
—**Michael Moebes (class of 2003)**

"A business plan is of the utmost importance. I don't see how [a solo can succeed] without one. It doesn't have to be super-formal. Just a basic budget; things like how much expenditures you will be making each month, how much money you need to cover those expenses, how much you need to cover overhead, and to bring home a decent salary." —**Paul Scott (class of 2008)**

"I kept my business plan pretty simple, and continue to develop it to this day. To me, a business plan should be a growing organism that takes account of your expanding knowledge and experience base. Sometimes, the simple act of committing your plans to writing can help to ensure that you follow through on those plans. Of course, a business plan is only as effective as your willingness to stick to it. Therefore, merely making a plan is only the first step in starting your law firm, and will do nothing by itself." —**Kevin Afghani (class of 2004)**

"[A business plan] is a roadmap for your practice's future. It doesn't have to be fancy or follow any formal outline; nor does it be more than a set of bullet points. All it needs to do is outline what you are going to do, with whom you are going to do it, and how you are going to do it. But don't just write it and put it away. Refer to it regularly, and update it when necessary. But stay focused on your original purpose. Without a road map, you won't know how to get there . . . or know when you've arrived." —**Bruce Cameron (class of 2007)**

"I worked for two years on my business plan before I opened my practice, and I am very glad I did. Without it, I think it would have taken four to six months to turn a profit; with the plan, I made a profit within two months after opening and in every month since."
—**Dean N. Alterman (class of 1989)**

"I think it's very important for me to put things on paper. Frankly, I haven't followed most of what I wrote in my first business plan, but it was a really useful exercise. And the financial part of it is incredibly important so you can budget if things don't take off for a while."
—**Matthew G. Kaiser (class of 2002)**

"Whether you draft a traditional, formal business plan, or spend just a few pages outlining your goals and expectations, you really should have some plan in place . . . and review it and update it regularly (say, every six months). Without one, it would be like driving across country without a map. Sure, you may eventually get to your destination, but it won't be by the most direct or effective route." —**Jan M. Tamanini (class of 1984)**

"It certainly makes life easier to know where you are going, so you'll know when you get there. Setting reasonable goals and monitoring progress for yourself gives you a chance to see how your practice evolves, and gives you the opportunity to sit back, reflect, and determine if opportunities exist in other practice areas which might be a good fit for your personality and comfort zone." —**Bruce L. Dorner (class of 1977)**

"It is critical to have a business plan, but also to keep it updated. Your plans for your practice will change as you get more into it, so you have to keep your business plan fluid and refer back to it. It's a document for you to lay out your plans and goals. Take it to a small business center or SCORE office and have them give you feedback on it. It can't hurt." —**Stephanie Kimbro (class of 2003)**

"I think a business plan is crucial. It keeps you on track, and is a great tool to make decisions efficiently. A friend who owns an ad agency explained the best use of a business plan: when you're making a decision about your business, see if [the decision] would complement or hinder your company's purpose as outlined in your business plan. If [the decision] hinders it, don't do it."
—**Gina Bongiovi (class of 2007)**

"I don't think a traditional, written-out business plan is too important. But you should certainly have a clear idea of what you want, and how you are going to do it. [Before I began], a few people grilled me about business and financial projections. But the truth is you can't really project what business might be like in the beginning. So, for certain aspects of going solo, it's more about adaptation than planning."
—**Adam Neufer (class of 2009)**

How important is a business plan?

Some highly disciplined solos spend several weeks writing their business plan, researching practice areas, identifying potential competitors, and setting milestones for revenues. Others just dive into practice with no idea of where they're headed. Whether you develop a business plan or not is your choice; the only scenario where it is essential, though, is if you intend to apply for a bank loan (which isn't recommended and shouldn't be necessary if you keep overhead low).

Of the various components of a traditional business plan, the "mission statement" is essential, and calls for you to calculate as best you can your expected starting revenues and expenses, some ideas on how you might attract clients, and your revenue goals at various junctures: say, at six months, one year, and three years. As you draft your mission statement, be specific. Use the following questions to get you started:

WHO (a two-part question). Who are you (your background), and what type of clients do you want to serve?

WHAT. What kind of law will your firm focus on? What makes your firm unique?

WHEN. Your business plan should include the date that you intend to open your doors. If you've already been in business for a while, note that as well.

WHERE. Identify where your firm will be located. Will you have offices in different cities?

HOW. How will you serve clients? In your office? Will you offer advice by phone or e-mail? How will you use technology to serve your practice?

Some additional considerations:

Have you done a SWOT analysis? A SWOT analysis (Strengths, Weaknesses, Opportunities, Threats) is a strategic planning tool to evaluate the potential viability of a business venture. It's not typically included in law firm business plan templates, but it is a quick way to focus your planning efforts.

What are your strengths? Focus on the competencies and advantages for which your firm has an edge.

What are your weaknesses? Consider the challenges that you face. If you're a new grad, you may have trouble pitching your services. Or perhaps there's an area where you've always wanted to practice but it's dominated by BigLaw firms. Listing your weaknesses can be discouraging, but it will force you to focus on ways to overcome these challenges.

What are your opportunities? Are there parts of the market that are underserved? Do you have a unique way to deliver legal services?

What are your possible threats? Maybe you want to handle personal injury cases but you live in a state where the political climate leans towards tort reform? Perhaps you practice in a highly competitive field. Devise a strategy for addressing those threats.

What is your marketing plan? How are you going to attract clients?

What is your expected revenue, and sources of revenue in the first few months? Don't be discouraged if the first few months reflect a big fat zero!

What are your projected expenses? You can also set milestones and goals for reaching certain income levels.

28. How important is a business plan?

"I don't think [a business plan] is very important. Sure, you should take pen to paper and get a general sense of what it will cost to open your doors, how much income you need to bring in, how soon you need income, etc. As a new solo, your business plan can be as simple as this: spend as little as you can, do everything you can do to market your business, and do a good job. That's the plan. If you do those things, you've done what you can to succeed."
—**Mark Tanney (class of 1998)**

"I didn't do one. I know you are supposed to, but I didn't. And I haven't missed it."
—**Lynda L. Hinkle (class of 2009)**

"Whether or not to write a business plan probably depends on experience level and practice area. For me, it was not important at all. At least, I didn't have one, and I wouldn't know how to write one. It's possible, though, that I might be vastly more wealthy and nearing financial security if I had had one. I guess ignorance is bliss."
—**Mitchell J. Matorin (class of 1993)**

"I didn't create a formal business plan before beginning. But several months ago, I did make a marketing plan for the year. It's been VERY helpful in keeping me motivated about marketing."
—**Sarah White (class of 2002)**

"I started [my practice] without a business plan, and I think I was held back because of it."
—**Marc W. Matheny (class of 1980)**

"Just keep records of your finances, and keep your expenses as low as possible. Once you hit your mark for the month, put the rest in savings."
—**Eric P. Ganci (class of 2008)**

29. What would you tell new solos about malpractice insurance?

"Absolutely positively get it. New or old solos need malpractice insurance."
—**Herb Dubin (class of 1964)**

"Buy it. You'll sleep better, and, hopefully, you won't need it. There are so many stressful aspects to running your own business and being a solo practitioner that it just makes sense to take this one off the list and insure this risk."
—**Cailie A. Currin (class of 1988)**

"Get it. You've got enough on your mind without worrying about [a malpractice claim]. And [the insurance] probably isn't as expensive as you think for a new attorney, and it will give you real peace of mind." —**Mitchell J. Matorin (class of 1993)**

"Buy it. In large amounts."
—**Kara O'Donnell (class of 1995)**

"Get it." —**Michael Moebes (class of 2003)**

"Get it." —**Eric P. Ganci (class of 2008)**

"Just get it! It's not that expensive."
—**Paul Scott (class of 2008)**

"It's way cheaper than you think."
—**Matthew G. Kaiser (class of 2002)**

"Absolutely essential. Dealing with the public is unpredictable. Protect yourself at all costs."
—**Abbe W. McClane (class of 2003)**

"The main risk is the cost of defense if someone brings a complaint. In DC [malpractice insurance] is not required, but I have it mainly to protect my family. It's not necessarily the first priority, but I think it is probably a good idea to get insurance as soon as you can." —**Mark Tanney (class of 1998)**

How important is malpractice insurance?

One absolute rule I have for new solos is that they must purchase malpractice insurance. In the interest of full disclosure, I admit to not following my own advice during my first three years of practice! Back then, I was young and cocky, and I calculated that my potential exposure was low given my regulatory practice, my "long shot" litigation matters and criminal defense work. I assumed legal malpractice insurance was as costly as health insurance and probably couldn't afford it. I had a nothing-to-lose attitude back then, figuring that if anyone sued me I'd simply pack up my firm and walk away. I see things differently now.

Here are some of the factors you should consider in purchasing malpractice insurance as well as suggestions on how to procure the best plan for your firm:

Does your state require malpractice coverage or have a mandatory disclosure policy? You may not even have a choice about whether to get legal malpractice insurance. In fact, Oregon, requires all lawyers to buy malpractice insurance. And seven other states—Arkansas, California, New Hampshire, New Mexico, Ohio, Pennsylvania and South Dakota—require attorneys to reveal to prospective clients whether they have malpractice coverage, while 11 other states require insurance disclosure on lawyers' annual registration statements (which, depending upon the state, are potentially available to the public).

Do you need malpractice insurance for business opportunities? Another factor to consider is whether you need malpractice coverage for business opportunities. Some referral services will not refer cases to lawyers who do not carry sufficient malpractice coverage. Many times, an RFP (request for proposal) for legal services also requires coverage. Even law firms and attorneys who retain lawyers for per diem or contract work often require some amount of malpractice coverage.

How much does your degree of exposure matter? Your own assessment of your degree of malpractice exposure should not serve as the deciding factor in your decision regarding coverage. Even though the chances are low of a client actually winning a malpractice action against you and collecting a judgment, it doesn't take much for a client to initiate such an action in hopes of pressuring a quick settlement—or worse, to file a bar complaint which, if unfavorably resolved, can cause damage to your reputation and lead to a suspension. Malpractice insurance buys you the peace of mind; one less thing to worry

"Check with your local bar; it may be a requirement. If it's not, get it anyway. It helps you sleep at night. Besides, most malpractice insurance providers are good for a free ethics CLE or two, and they are usually quite willing to help you design good workable practice management solutions that can help reduce your premium.

The only problem with malpractice insurance is figuring out how much coverage is needed. My provider told me to imagine what an average claim might be and get enough coverage to cover two claims per year. In the end, I chose the most coverage I could afford."
—**Bruce Cameron (class of 2007)**

about when that client who started out so reasonably starts threatening a grievance. Moreover, if your risk of exposure is low anyway, you'll probably be able to find a relatively inexpensive coverage plan.

How do you purchase malpractice insurance?

Many state bar associations have an insurance company that is designated as a "preferred provider" or bar association sponsor. Be wary of these designations; it's no guarantee that the company offers the lowest cost or is the most reliable. To find potential malpractice companies, seek advice from other attorneys who have personally procured the plan and who practice in the same jurisdiction. Sensitive to the growing number of lawyers going solo in a weakened economy, many carriers now offer extremely affordable policies—as little as $500/year—to solos just out of school or in their first year of practice. Other carriers discount policies for part-time practices, based on number of hours worked and/or income earned. Once you've gathered a list of two or three prospective providers, shop around for quotes. If you don't want to do the legwork yourself, work with an insurance broker, or get referrals from colleagues or your local bar. A section of the ABA's Web site (www.americanbar.org) is dedicated to the purchase of malpractice insurance.

"It's not cheap, but what insurance is? Shop around. I got a good deal by not going with the first quote I got." **—Lynda L. Hinkle (class of 2009)**

"Get it. Shop around, but get malpractice insurance immediately."
—Marc W. Matheny (class of 1980)

"Shop around. Don't allocate more than 5% [of coverage] to any practice area you're not telling people you handle. For example, if you plan to be a family lawyer but might do a few estate plans, give the family law section 95% and the estate planning section 5%. I was told that anything over 5% or 10% triggers a new practice area and increases your premiums. I was also assured that if you are sued for something outside your listed practice areas, you're still covered by the insurance. So don't increase your premiums unnecessarily." **—Gina Bongiovi (class of 2007)**

"Buy it. Just don't buy more than you need. Above all, watch carefully, take your time, and the need to notify your carrier will be reduced."
—Bruce L. Dorner (class of 1977)

"Research, research, research! Make sure you understand the provisions of the policy and the coverage. Pay attention to indemnification clauses; whether the provider can settle without your consent; whether you can choose your own defense counsel; and the amount of coverage for each claim and the aggregate coverage."
—Adam Neufer (class of 2009)

"The decision as to whether to purchase malpractice insurance depends heavily on your State Bar rules and the clients you intend to serve. Speaking for myself, I waited to get malpractice insurance until I felt it was necessary. In particular, I was talking to potential clients that required me to have malpractice insurance. In that situation, I felt it was worth the investment."
—Kevin Afghani (class of 2004)

"If you unbundle legal services or use technology in your practice, understand what is and is not covered in the malpractice policy regarding

29. What would you tell new solos about malpractice insurance?

30. What role does social media play in marketing your practice and building relationships?

coverage of hardward and software. Educate your carrier about what you are using and discuss it with them." —**Stephanie Kimbro (class of 2003)**

"You can do without until you get a regular cash flow." —**Thomas J. Crane (class of 1983)**

"It really depends on your practice area and who your clients are. I flew without anything in my first 16 months of practice. Doing mostly transactional work and working mostly with people I had known before, I didn't feel too exposed. I put it off until the middle of my second year. In the end, the online solo community helped me to make my decision on how much and with whom to insure."
—**Jan M. Tamanini (class of 1984)**

"I do quite a bit of marketing through social media, and I spend significant resources on marketing." —**Cailie A.Currin (class of 1988)**

"My blog is a good marketing tool. Although I am on a number of LinkedIn Groups and have a Twitter account, I don't really use them. I find listservs more helpful."
—**Nina Kallen (class of 2003)**

"I have a Web site, a blog, a Facebook fan page, and a Twitter account. I have gotten many clients from my Web site, and from referrals from friends who remembered I was a lawyer because they read my last "status update" on Facebook." —**Paul Scott (class of 2008)**

"Facebook has been a major marketing tool and LinkedIn a minor one. And while I don't tweet often, I do tweet." —**Lynda L. Hinkle (class of 2009)**

"I have made a lot of contacts (and money) from networking and advertising on Facebook!"
—**Jenee Oliver (class of 2005)**

"I keep a Twitter and Facebook account because they provide an easy way to quickly share information with clients, and they provide a way for potential clients to interact with me. I also learn from colleagues by monitoring their Twitter and Facebook pages."
—**Tonya Coles (class of 2006)**

"Social media makes practicing more affordable in that you can get your message out faster and cheaper than old fashioned print ads and articles." —**Kara O'Donnell (class of 1995)**

"[Social media] plays a huge role. But it's such a new area, and the Courts haven't determined

exactly how to approach it. Know your rules regarding solicitations, especially since others can repost your content across the Internet."
—**Eric P. Ganci (class of 2008)**

"Social media has been a godsend. I've revamped my Web site and promote my blog on Facebook and Twitter. According to my monthly Google Analytics reports, the majority of visits to my site consistently come from Twitter. Just last week I was meeting a referral source at a coffee shop. I was approached by a guy who recognized me from Twitter and said, 'Hey! You're LawyerGina!' I was shocked." —**Gina Bongiovi (class of 2007)**

"I have not derived any cases from Facebook or Twitter . . . yet. But am sure I will. The marketing reach of online social media is remarkable."
—**Thomas J. Crane (class of 1983)**

"I've had good experiences with LinkedIn and similar online networking sites, and appearing on Avvo and Cornell's Legal Information Institute has brought me some clients. I don't use Facebook for my practice, and I'm on Twitter but admit to not tweeting very regularly."
—**Jan M. Tamanini (class of 1984)**

"[Social media plays] a very big role. I didn't start doing it because someone said I needed to; I was already doing it for fun, and parlayed it into online networking for law. [In my opinion, though] attorneys who start using social media because they're told to at a weekend marketing conference are [often] awful at it, and are wasting their time."
—**Michael Moebes (class of 2003)**

"[Social media] plays a significant role; not in generating clients, but in letting clients know that I am out there and in the environment.

[In my opinion] seeing press, media, and even self-generated blogs, gives clients comfort that you at least are engaged and involved in your practice." —**Jeffrey G. Neu (class of 2006)**

"Social media is a great way to reconnect with old networks or contacts, and keep them informed about your current practice. When I started my practice, I became friends on Facebook with everyone I knew from high school, college, law school, and work. And I used my Facebook—and LinkedIn —connections to build my contact and referral list. I have received a handful of referrals this way, so [social media] has yielded some tangible benefit. I'm not sure how much benefit this is seeking out new contacts through Facebook, so I always make sure that I know a person outside of Facebook before making that person a Facebook "friend."
—**Kevin Afghani (class of 2004)**

"[Social media] just isn't for me. I didn't like blogging or Twittering, and I started resenting the time I supposed to spend online. I don't think there are any straight lines to getting clients. If you enjoy working your social media angles, do that; if you prefer having lunch with people, or talking to clients, or going to CLE's, do that instead. If you're going solo, it's important to be yourself. If you're not the kind of person who is going to enjoy using social media, cut yourself some slack and don't do it." —**Matthew G. Kaiser (class of 2002)**

"I think social media is a poor marketing tool. It requires a lot of time, and it has a poor ROI. Social media is not a big part of my marketing, BUT it does play a role in maintaining contact with other lawyers, and provides an informal network of mentors and a body of supportive presences with whom to commiserate, bounce ideas off, and to act as a calming presence. It can also be useful to maintain contact with established clients; but as for finding new clients, [social media] is only slightly more efficient than shouting down a well. There are simply too many competing voices for all but the most persistent new voices to be heard above the din. [In my opinion], social media is about constantly feeding the beast with new and ever-changing content while good marketing is about getting the same message (perhaps with slight variations) out there with clockwork regularity." —**Bruce Cameron (class of 2007)**

"I'm still in the start-up phase, so profitability is still a goal. I'm just happy when I've broken even at the end of a month." —**Bruce Cameron (class of 2007)**

"I budget very carefully, and say 'no' a lot." —**Marc W. Matheny (class of 1980)**

"I review my profit-and-loss statements on a monthly basis, as well as attempt to accurately project the anticipated work load coming up." —**Jeffrey G. Neu (class of 2006)**

"I review my hourly rate and flat-fee structure on a yearly basis, and I am careful to build expenses and taxes into my fees." —**Tonya Coles (class of 2006)**

"I budget my annual marketing expenses ahead of time and try to stick with that plan. I save in the months when there are more clients for those months that will be dry. I also am strict about keep up with online marketing; working on it today for the clients that it will bring in six months from now. [Marketing] is a never-ending process . . . but it helps to maintain profitability." —**Stephanie Kimbro (class of 2003)**

"I was able to rely on some contract patent work in order to supplement my income. I calculated my monthly personal and business expenses, and tried to control the flow of incoming contract patent work based on the amount that I needed to pay my monthly expenses." —**Kevin Afghani (class of 2004)**

"I don't spend money until I can afford it, and I keep up with my marketing efforts. For example, I attend a monthly luncheon that's been my biggest

revenue generator, and have approached the head of the group about presenting during a luncheon to get more exposure."
—**Gina Bongiovi (class of 2007)**

"You have to be flexible [to stay profitable]. I started accepting family law cases, even though I would rather not. But you have to pay bills while working those contingency cases."
—**Thomas J. Crane (class of 1983)**

"[The key to profitability] is marketing, marketing, marketing. It doesn't matter if you're having one of the most profitable months or the worst month. Taking a certain amount of time out to market yourself (networking lunches, ads, etc.), will ensure that your name is fresh on people's minds when they need an attorney."
—**Paul Scott (class of 2008)**

"[Profitability]? Work hard, work efficiently, work long hours."—**Herb Dubin (class of 1964)**

"[How to maintain profitability]? I look at my skinny kids, and I take time to evaluate what has worked and what hasn't in terms of generating revenue." —**Michael Moebes (class of 2003)**

"In addition to the standard networking, I check in with current clients, friends, and business contacts on a somewhat regular basis to ask if there's anything they might need in the way of the services that I provide . . . or if they know anyone who may be in need of my services. It's hard at first to ask directly for referrals, but it really pays dividends. At first I didn't have the best budgeting setup; I was sort of winging it as I went along. I now plan for my expenses, and if I'm not bringing in the income I grit my teeth and defer things that

aren't absolute necessities. I also regularly review recurring costs to see whether they are worth what I'm paying, and investigate alternatives."
—**Jan M. Tamanini (class of 1984)**

"Keep looking for new and returning clients, and don't purchase anything that won't either make you more productive or free up more time to take in more clients."—**Bruce L. Dorner (class of 1977)**

"Keep your expenses low, and keep marketing to bring in clients to increase income. It's that simple." —**Gabriel Cheong (class of 2007)**

"I do not have a Plan B. This is my passion, and I plan to do this for the rest of my working career."**—Cailie A. Currin (class of 1988)**

"I've never had a Plan B. But if I see [things] aren't working out, I'll work on one. Until then, all my time, energy, and focus is going into Plan A"
—Paul Scott (class of 2008)

"[Plan B]? The question is totally wrong. I have the greatest job security of almost any lawyer that I know. The only person who can fire me is me"
—Marc W. Matheny (class of 1980)

"Plan B? See Plan A."
—Mitchell J. Matorin (class of 1993)

"Frankly, I don't have a Plan B. In the present economy, running a solo practice is the only appealing career option that is actually open to me." **—Mark Tanney (class of 1998)**

"If I am only meant to walk the solo path for a brief period, I am still richer for the experience. And should I have to close the door to my practice, I guess I would head back to the job market a little

more experienced than when I left it."
—Bruce Cameron (class of 2007)

"I shudder to think of it, but failure is always a possibility. However, having tasted the nectar of freedom, I would look for a high level of autonomy in any new position." **—Kevin Afghani (class of 2004)**

"If things don't work out I would probably go back to work in an established firm. Or maybe create another type of business because I love being an entrepreneur!" **—Sarah White (class of 2002)**

"[Plan B]? Consult, teach, do whatever needs to be done." **—Abbe W. McClane (class of 2003)**

"I have a JD/MBA, so I would come back as a business strategy consultant. Or work as a sommelier, or in a culinary school. I'm a Libra; I can't decide these things."
—Gina Bongiovi (class of 2007)

"[Plan B]? Rent a time machine, so I can take myself back to when I was filling out law school applications and punch myself in the face."
—Eric P. Ganci (class of 2008)

PART FOUR:
Reflections

32. Would you still solo given
what you've learned?

32. Where do you see the practice
of law, and solo'ing, headed?

*C*onventional wisdom holds that when we reflect on our lives we're more likely to regret what we didn't do than what we did.

    Lots of lawyers dream about starting a firm; some of them even take a few steps forward by drafting a business plan or looking at office space. But in the end, their circumstances (a spouse losing a job), their practicality (I hate my job, but I don't want to give up my paycheck), or their fear of the unknown keep them from making the leap. Without question, starting your own law firm is not easy; in fact, it just might be one of the toughest professional decisions you ever make. But you can take comfort in this: the dozens of solos cited in this Companion Guide once stood at the same precipice where you are now, and most of them took the leap without regret.

    As the legal profession goes through some very challenging times, with corporate clients refusing to pay BigLaw's sky-high rates, and jobs being offshored or replaced by technology, the solos quoted below are excited and optimistic about the opportunities that lay ahead.

"I'm glad I decided to solo, and I would do it all over again. My practice and my life are more interesting as a result."
—**David Abeshouse (class of 1982)**

"I wake up loving what I do every day. I look forward to Fridays as much as Mondays."
—**Gabriel Cheong (class of 2007)**

"Given what I've learned, I wish I would have gone solo sooner. I'm enjoying practicing law more than ever, and hope that I am fortunate enough to have my own practice for as long as I practice law."
—**Kevin Afghani (class of 2004)**

"I'm having a great time doing what I'm doing. I look forward to it every day. I can't wait to get to my desk in the morning. I'm not yet on solid ground financially. But I'll always be glad I [solo'd] no matter how it turns out." —**Mark Tanney (class of 1998)**

"[Solo again]? Yes, in a heartbeat."
—**Matthew G. Kaiser (class of 2002)**

"Yes, but it would have been nice [if I would have] had a fund set up prior to going solo."
—**Kara O'Donnell (class of 1995)**

"No regrets at all." —**Mitchell J. Matorin (class of 1993)**

"Unquestionably and undeniably, without reservation." —**Marc W. Matheny (class of 1980)**

"Heck yeah!"—**Thomas J. Crane (class of 1983)**

"Yes. I'm the best boss I've ever had: tough but fair!" —**Jan M. Tamanini (class of 1984)**

"I absolutely would choose to solo again. For all the financial uncertainty and moments of being

33. Would you still solo given what you've learned?

34. Where do you see the practice of law, and solo'ing, headed?

overwhelmed by workload and isolation, there are so many more moments of satisfaction and freedom." —**D. Jill Pugh (class of 1994)**

"Absolutely. Everyone in the world told me that the first year . . . even the first two years . . . can be very slow. And they were right. But six months into going solo, my phone rang constantly, and I got a steady stream of higher quality referrals, I have interesting work, and I enjoy what I'm doing."
—**Sergio Benavides (class of 2005)**

"I will always have doubts about my decision to go solo, but in the final analysis it has been a fantastic learning experience. Whether or not I succeed as a solo, I am glad to be traveling this path." —**Bruce Cameron (class of 2007)**

"I love getting up every day to go to the office. I like being able to choose my cases, and how I am going to handle them. It is certainly a sacrifice to go solo, but the sacrifice will pay off in dividends if done right." —**Paul Scott (class of 2008)**

"Although it was the right decision given my circumstances at the time, I would have preferred to start my career at a multi-lawyer firm and then go solo after becoming more seasoned. But I do not regret the decision."
—**Adam Neufer (class of 2009)**

"I'm still not making the money I want, but my freedom is invaluable. The mere thought of going to work for a firm where my hours are tracked, where my bonuses are poached by senior partners, where I have no say in what clients I have to take, and where I have to beg for days off, makes me queasy. I'm doing the best I can, and the money will come. I just have to be patient."
—**Gina Bongiovi (class of 2007)**

"I see solo and small firms continuing to leverage their flexibility and adaptability in ways that would be hard to do for large firms."
—**Jeffrey G. Neu (class of 2007)**

"I think that solos and small firms are going to blossom, picking up where some of the antiquated big firms are losing clients."
—**Lynda L. Hinkle (class of 2009)**

"I think there is a big future for solo and small firm law. The BigLaw business model seems to be fading. [In the future], prospective clients using Internet resources will be able to solve routine legal problems on their own. But they will still need lawyers for issues they cannot resolve for themselves. Solo lawyers can succeed, but they will need to be highly sensitive to what clients actually need lawyers to do."
—**Mark Tanney (class of 1998)**

"Solos are on the rise! BigLaw cannot continue to sustain its practices in this changing legal marketplace. Trends in outsourcing of legal services and the globalization of law firms are all going to encourage the growth of niche solo practices that cross geographic boundaries. I also think that in the next decade most solos will have to have some virtual component to their practice given the consumer demand for online legal services whether it's just communicating online or full-blown online delivery of legal services. It's an exciting and optimistic time to be a solo."
—**Stephanie Kimbro (class of 2003)**

"So much of society and the practice of law is changing because of economic and political turmoil, technology, and social trends. But solo firms are well-positioned for times like these. We don't have committees or equity partners to answer to, and, if it becomes necessary, we can make changes to our way of doing business very quickly."– **Cailie A. Currin (class of 1988)**

"[In my opinion], the practice of law is swinging towards an era of solo and small firm practices because of their flexibility and ability to innovate. It will be the solo/smalls who evolve their practices to fill niches as they become available, and to respond to the ebb & flow of the practice of law. We are facing a period of time where we have a glut of lawyers. My guess is that most of the attrition will come from those firms that would fund their operation by borrowing on their accounts receivable, followed closely by those who maintain rigid adherence to the billable hour fee model. This may not be an extinction event, but you can see it from here."
—**Bruce Cameron (class of 2007)**

"I hear from many people who are downsizing and much happier patronizing a small business than giving their money to a conglomerate. [For this reason], I'm optimistic that smaller law firms will gain increasing credibility among clients small and large who have previously been ignored or taken for granted by BigLaw."
—**Gina Bongiovi (class of 2007)**

"I think that the practice of law will continue to evolve towards more efficient billing and management models. By their very nature, solos are at the forefront of this movement because we have the capability to design our own billing models, and to make our own choices in regard to law practice and file management. The public benefits from our efficient and effective legal representation."—**Brian M. Annino (class of 2003)**

"The legal field is going to take a huge amount of time to recover from all of the downsizing by larger firms. Once the field recovers, I think most of those who were forced into solo or small practice are going to keep what they have built. [As a result], this is going to create more competition amongst solo and smaller firms, and force them to find ways to evolve their billing methods."
—**Adam Neufer (class of 2009)**

"I'd like to think that things will continue to head in a more collaborative direction, with fewer big fights and more cooperation between parties who might otherwise come out swinging. And I'm also optimistic that alternative fee structures will become more the norm than hourly billing. I think solos have a great benefit to offer their clients. But we have to learn to market ourselves not as selling pieces of paper, but selling advice and services, with documents as a byproduct of that advice."
—**Jan M. Tamanini (class of 1984)**

"Small firm practice is going to be around for as long as I can tell. There is an abundance of both business and individual clients who prefer the personal attention that a smaller firm can offer . . . with the same or higher caliber work of a bigger firm." —**Paul Scott (class of 2008)**

"The solo and small firm practice is the future in my area (patent preparation and prosecution). Clients can have assurance that the lawyer with whom they are dealing will be the lawyer who is actually performing the work."
—**Kevin Afghani (class of 2004)**

"Big firm layoffs and increasing client cost pressure have opened up new opportunities for solos and small firms to take a piece of the

work that always went to the big firms by default. [For this reason], I think the last few years have been transformative for the solo/small firm practice. I'm fairly hopeful about the future of solo/small firm practice generally and about my own prospects specifically."
—**Mitchell J. Matorin (class of 1993)**

"Like all businesses, the truly hungry [solos] will be in it for the long haul. The meek will move into paycheck jobs. I have hope for me; if I don't, who will?" —**Kara O'Donnell (class of 1995)**

"There will always be room for the very large firms, because only they can put dozens of lawyers to work on a big case or a big transaction. Think of them as gigantic 'cruise ships'. But there will also always be room for solos and small firms, run by lawyers who choose to do a few things very well and very efficiently. Think of us as 'speedboats'. The cruise ships carry more people further, but the speed boats carry a few people faster, and can go up little streams from which the cruise ships are locked out."
—**Dean N. Alterman (class of 1989)**

PART FIVE:
Solos by Choice: The Expanded Profiles

1. Kevin Afghani (Class of 2004)

2. Gina Bongiovi (Class of 2007)

3. Bruce Cameron (Class of 2007)

4. Lynda L. Hinkle (Class of 2009)

5. Mitchell J. Matorin (Class of 1993)

6. Kara O'Donnell (Class of 1995)

7. Paul Scott (Class of 2008)

8. Jan M. Tamanini (Class of 1984)

9. Mark Tanney (Class of 1998)

1. Kevin Afghani

KEVIN AFGHANI
Education: Tulane School of Law; Class of 2004
Resume: Practicing law 5 years.
Solo practice: Two years
Practice specialty: Patent law

Q: Why did you decide to solo?
"Before starting a solo patent practice, I was an IP associate in BigLaw. The money was good, but after about a year I realized it was not a good fit. If I wanted a fulfilling legal practice, I would have to escape. Going solo has exceeded my expectations in every way imaginable. I feel in control of my destiny, and my future no longer depends upon the whims of a partner."

Q: What sacrifices did you make to solo?
"I gave up a BigLaw salary and a regular paycheck for no guaranteed income at no guaranteed time. [The sacrifice] was worth every penny."

Q: How did you explain your decision to colleagues?
"Some people excel in a BigLaw environment, others in a more structured government or in-house environment. I was cut out for solo practice because I like being my own boss, and because I have a high tolerance for risk."

Q: What did you know about solo'ing before you began?
"Everything I knew about solo'ing was based on observing colleagues who had gone on their own. I knew that every aspect of running a business would fall upon me, and I knew about the risks involved."

Q: What about the risks in a solo practice?
"One of the most important personality traits of a solo practitioner is a high tolerance for risk.

If you are uncomfortable with not getting paid for over a month or two, and not being able to accurately project your income —at least in the starting phase —you should think seriously about your decision to solo. Indeed, the risk factor is the main force preventing many of my colleagues from breaking out on their own."

Q: What about job security?
"When you work for a law firm, you derive income from a single source, and it can lull you into a false sense of security simply because you're receiving a paycheck at regular intervals. But going solo can actually increase your job security by diversifying the sources from which you derive income."

Q: What role does a spouse/partner play in a solo's success?
"My fiancé was critical in my decision to go solo. To this day I do not think I would've done it without her support. Since she herself is a patent attorney, she understood very well the stresses that come with being in a law firm. She saw the perfect fit between me and solo practice even before I myself had realized it."

Q: What was your biggest goof, and what did it teach you?
"Early on, I failed to identify my ideal type of client or focus my efforts on acquiring this ideal type of client. Instead, my business development efforts tended to follow a scattershot approach."

Q: What are the biggest challenges when you're the boss?
"You need to establish a budget for insurance (health, dental, malpractice, disability), and any of the other services normally provided by an employer. Second, set up a time management and appointment system, because you will have

to wear many different hats on any given day, including collector, lawyer, accountant, PR expert, or janitor."

Q: How important is a business plan?
"To me, a business plan should be a growing organism that takes account of your expanding knowledge and experience base. [In the beginning], I kept my business plan pretty simple, and I continue to develop it to this day. Sometimes, the simple act of committing your plans to writing can help to ensure that you follow through on those plans."

Q: How important are people skills in a solo's success?
"People skills are an absolute necessity. When I look at how much my personal interactions have increased since going solo, I don't see how it would be possible without being able to effectively interact with others. For someone trying to build a client base from the ground up, you will be interacting with others extensively. People skills should be developed or practiced."

Q: What business skills are essential?
"Unless you're planning on hiring a CPA, you should gain at least some basic knowledge in federal income tax to ensure that you are not over- or under- paying your taxes. I was pretty freaked out to learn that I was required to pay a quarterly estimated tax to the IRS based on my projected income, and that my failure to pay this quarterly estimated tax could result in an underpayment penalty."

Q: Any advice for new solos?
"If you are soloing with little or no experience, you might explore project-partnering with an experienced lawyer in your practice area. They will be able to provide you with referrals and the mentoring you need. Of course, they will also probably require you to share fees with them, but this financial sacrifice could yield long-term benefits. I recommend partnering with an attorney who allows you to have direct contact with clients for which you perform work."

Q: Kevin, given what you've learned, would you still solo?
"I wish I'd have gone solo sooner. I'm enjoying practicing law more than ever, and hope that I am fortunate enough to have my own practice for as long as I practice law."

GINA BONGIOVI

Education: University of Nevada/Las Vegas, JD/
MBA; Class of 2007

Solo practice: Two years

Practice specialty: Part-time general counsel for
small businesses

Q: Why did you decide to solo?

"In my second year of law school, one of my
professors described the typical life of a new
attorney: it was the polar opposite of what I'd
attended law school to become. From then on, I
knew I wanted to solo. I couldn't imagine toiling
away four years of a part-time law program while
working full or part-time, only to lose some of
the freedom I'd enjoyed before enrolling in law
school."

Q: Is there a solo type?

"The successful solo must have self-discipline!
You don't have a supervisor breathing down your
neck or a time card to punch. No one is taking
issue with your billable hour quota, and you don't
have a paycheck direct-deposited to your account
every two weeks. You have to manage your time,
manage your caseload, make your own schedule,
and handle all the administrative stuff, too. Some
people just don't have the desire to shoulder
that much responsibility. And that's okay. Just be
honest with yourself about your personality and
your motivations, or you'll be a miserable square
peg in a round hole."

**Q: What are your sharpest memories
of starting out?**

"It was a rough time. For the first eight months, I
waited with almost unbearable anticipation for the
phone to ring. When it did, I felt like hiding under
my desk. I was stuck between the excitement of
building my business and terror that I would screw

something up. For a few months, the fear was
almost paralyzing. I'd find myself in tears some
days, wondering what I'd done, whether I'd made
the right decision to start my own firm, or to even
attend law school."

Q: What sacrifices did you make to solo?

"Money is the first and most significant sacrifice.
Two years in and I'm still not making the money I
want. However, I chose to laser-focus my practice
area, and I don't dabble in other areas. This way,
I have sacrificed a lot in potential revenue, but I
have also become the go-to person for my practice
area. And even though clients don't come along as
often, the clients I do get now are higher quality."

**Q: What role does a spouse/partner
play in a solo's success?**

"If it wasn't for my husband's support, I wouldn't
have been able to go on my own. The financial hit
we took while I got the firm started wasn't easy,
and the emotional turmoil I put myself through
wasn't easy either. Watching me vacillate between
elation and terror was pretty rough on him
because he couldn't really do anything to help."

Q: What frustrations are solos likely to experience?

"My biggest frustration was, and still is, the
realization that law school did nothing to prepare
me for actual practice. I thought for sure that
toiling those three years under constant stress
and anxiety would provide the knowledge I
needed to practice law. I am just amazed how
precious little I learned about real-life litigation in
law school, and that feeling has not waned."

**Q: What do you like/dislike about
the autonomy of solo practice?**

"I love the autonomy [of being a solo]. It means
being able to take care of a friend after surgery,

being able to attend my nephew's basketball game, being able to take my dog to the vet."

Q: What role do mentors play in your practice?
"Books and CLE's can take you only so far. Mentors and contacts are invaluable. A mentor can help you brainstorm ideas, guide you in making decisions, and keep you from falling on your face. Finding a mentor can be a challenge. But once a potential mentor walks into your life, show your appreciation and ask if you can lean on them for help. Most will find it flattering and a very rewarding way of giving back."

Q: What role do people skills play in your practice?
"People skills are crucial. Most solos are the face of their firm in marketing efforts and must be accessible and approachable. No matter your practice area, you will do some amount of counseling and deal with people's emotions. Having the skills to manage your reactions and keep the client calm will serve you well."

Q: What role does risk play in a solo practice?
"Risk is the ever-present ghost over your shoulder. From month to month, you can't rely on a steady income. You don't know if your clients will pay; you don't know if the phone will ring; you don't know if any consultation will turn into a client; you don't know if your particular niche will be eliminated due to some new legislation. Risk is probably the biggest factor in a solo practice. The trick is to figure out how to manage it, strategically and emotionally, so that dips don't sideline you, and you don't overspend in the good months. Budgeting is a great tool, as is having a solid business plan that you revisit every few months to make sure you're on the right track."

Q: What would you say to new solos about marketing? "
"Advertising is usually a waste of money unless you have a war chest to throw at a campaign designed to put your name in front of people at least seven times. Instead, I find networking to be the most profitable. Not just any networking, though. I spun my wheels in networking groups for about six months, signing very few clients because I was marketing to the wrong audience . . . potential clients. Now, I network and market to my referral sources, and it has made all the difference."

Q: What's your advice to new law grads who want to solo?
"Be prepared for the fear . . . market like crazy when business is slow . . . stay in contact with everyone you meet . . . don't be a general practitioner unless you're in a small town . . . keep your expenses low . . . and be honest with yourself: not everyone is cut out for having their own practice. You'll be miserable if you try to be a business owner when you might be happiest as an employee."

Q: What about job security?
"I see friends who worked as loyal employees for over a decade laid off with an hour's notice. No one these days has any job security. I might go so far as to argue the highest degree of job security is enjoyed by the self-employed."

Q: Would you still solo given what you've learned?
"I'm still not making the money I want, but my freedom is invaluable. The mere thought of going to work for a firm where my hours are tracked, where my bonuses are poached by senior

partners, where I have no say in what clients I have to take, and where I have to beg for days off, makes me queasy. I'm doing the best I can, and the money will come. I just have to be patient."

Q: Gina, what's the future of the solo practice?
"I'm optimistic that smaller law firms will gain increasing credibility among clients small and large who have previously been ignored or taken for granted by BigLaw."

BRUCE CAMERON
Education: Hamline University School of Law;
    Class of 2007
Resume: Practicing law for three years;
    previously, a research scientist
Solo practice: Three years
Practice specialty: Collaborative family law,
    probate, and real estate work

Q: What role does a spouse/partner play in a solo's success?
"If it weren't for my wife's support, I don't think I would have made it through law school . . . much less have the courage to go solo."

Q: Why did you decide to solo?
"Going solo right out of law school, AND practicing in a small rural town, was the last thing I wanted to do. My plan had always been to find an associate position with a firm doing IP work. After all, what firm wouldn't want an experienced software engineer/biomedical researcher-with-multiple-graduate-degrees-turned-lawyer? As it turns out, hiring partners aren't much interested in an over-40, second career, 'night school' lawyer (actually, I took all my classes on the weekends) who graduated from a tier 3 school."

Q: What did you know about solo'ing before you began?
"I had no idea how complex a solo practice is, or that you that most of your time is spent on marketing and managing the business and a minority of time actually practicing law. Nor did I know that being a solo would be the scariest, most exhilarating, dullest, stimulating, stressful, challenging, satisfying thing I ever attempted."

Q: What role does risk play in a solo practice?
"Going solo means spending large amounts of

time and money in a venture with no defined return, and with odds that are undefined, unpredictable, and continuously variable! It's an intricate dance with risk . . . but not a gamble. [To manage risk], you need to think strategically, making decisions based on information and a cost/benefit analysis rather than reacting to immediate events. Risk is what makes my solo practice fun, exhilarating, worrisome . . . and scary at the same time. It's what keeps me sharp and drives me to do my best work."

Q: What are your sharpest memories of starting out?

"There was an intense rawness to those first days and months [of solo practice]. But my sharpest memories are more internal than external: the feeling of dread when I walked into the office each morning; the elation of that first client; the surprise when I got a referral; the exhilaration that came from getting a positive result for a client; and the contentment of earning that first fee."

Q: What sacrifices did you make to solo?

"It's not a 'sacrifice' as much as making trade-offs or substitutions. For example, date night for my wife and I changed from restaurants and theater tickets to take-out and a rented DVD. And those leisurely, two-week vacations are now a hectic three-day weekend."

Q: What are some of a solo's frustrations?

"Solo practitioners are the red-headed stepchildren of the legal profession. And the consensus is that if we were really good lawyers, we'd be working for one big firm or another. My frustration is with this persistent, subtle hostility. Beyond that, most of my daily frustrations are those any business experiences; clients who pay late and vendors who deliver late. But these are

transient frustrations, and can be corrected with the proper administration of chocolate, riding my horses, and —in extreme cases —Scotch."

Q: Can you solo on a shoestring budget?

"You can set up a solo office on a shoestring; you just can't run a solo practice on one. All those articles on the '$10,000 law practice', the '$5,000 law office', are correct as far as they go. But they don't consider what it costs to live AND maintain your practice. You need to factor in rent or mortgage payments, and those pesky bills for food, utilities, telephone, transportation, health insurance, and taxes. On top of that, costs for marketing, maintaining your license, and advancing court costs or filing fees on your client's behalf. On top of THAT, there are unexpected costs like the $500 brake job or the thousand-dollar medical bill."

Q: Any financial advice for new solos?

"You'll need an accountant at least three times during your first year: to set up your books and learn how to maintain them, to start planning for the year's taxes, and again at tax time."

Q: How you feel about business plans?

"It doesn't have to be fancy or follow any formal outline; nor does it have to be more than a set of bullet points. All it needs to do is outline what you are going to do, with whom you are going to do it, and how you are going to do it. But don't just write it and put it away. Refer to it regularly, and update it when necessary. But stay focused on your original purpose. Without a road map, you won't know how to get there . . . or know when you've arrived."

Q: What would you tell new lawyers about malpractice insurance?

"Check with your local bar; it may be a requirement. If it's not, get it anyway. It helps you sleep at night."

Q: What would you advise new solos about marketing?

"The more you know about your ideal client, and the more detailed description you have of that ideal client, the more cost-effective your marketing will be. Three suggestions: a) Tailor your marketing to your ideal client, and don't waste time, effort or money on methods that will not reach that ideal client . . . b) When preparing materials, you need to get across who you are, what you offer, why you should be hired, where you are located, and how to contact you in an efficient manner . . . and c) Have a uniform look across all your materials and a consistent presence. If you take an ad out in the local shopper, keep it going for several weeks, even months. Name recognition takes time and patience."

Q: Any other marketing advice?

"One big marketing *don't* concerns phone directory advertising. If you can't afford to put a full page ad on the cover, or in the front of the attorney's section, don't bother spending money on anything other than the minimal listing."

Q: What's your advice to new law grads?

"Have a mentor or two. Don't try to spread yourself across multiple practice areas. Focus on one and become competent in that field before adding additional practice areas. And attend all the CLE's in your practice area that you can afford."

Q: Bruce, what's the future for solo practices?

"The practice of law is swinging towards an era of solo and small firm practices because of their flexibility and ability to innovate. It will be the solo/smalls who evolve their practices to fill niches as they become available, and to respond to the ebb & flow of the practice of law. We are facing a period of time where we have a glut of lawyers. My guess is that most of the attrition will come from those firms that would fund their operation by borrowing on their accounts receivable, followed closely by those who maintain rigid adherence to the billable hour fee model. This may not be an extinction event, but you can see it from here."

LINDA HINKLE
Education: Rutgers University/Camden;
    Class of 2009
Resume: Practicing law for nearly two years;
    previously, teacher, writer, Congressional aide
Solo practice: One year
Practice specialties: Family, wills/estates,
    and small business

Q: Why did you decide to solo?
"Right before passing the bar I had a good, hard look at the situation—the economy, the competition for clerkships, a state hiring freeze—and I concluded that I might want to consider going out on my own. So, I asked someone I knew who [solo'd] right out of law school. He asked if I had chutzpah (well, actually, he asked me how big my balls were, but ya know. So, I told him very big!). He said I should be fine. So, from the time I passed the bar I started the process of going solo."

Q: What did you know about solo'ing before you began?
"I had some idea what was involved because I ran a business before. Other than that, I read a couple of books [about solo'ing], but that was it!"

Q: How did you explain your decision to your family?
"I didn't. I didn't explain myself to anyone except my husband, and I told him that I didn't want to hear any negative talk about [opening a solo practice]. I was just going to do it, and if it didn't work, we would worry about it then."

Q: How did you bring in a stream of revenue in the beginning?
"I started off with a few clients. It was enough to pay the bills in the office, which totaled under $1,000 a month. After the first month, I was able to start paying myself a salary. [Now] I spend half my time marketing/networking to keep bringing clients in."

Q: What are some of a solo's frustrations?
"Every day I start off thinking today is the day I am going to get caught up. By the time I've finished breakfast at my desk, that illusion is gone because four people called, my receptionist is telling me a fifth is on the line, and there are four emails requiring immediate attention (and hundreds that can wait)!"

Q: What role does risk play in the life of a solo?
"Every day is a risk. Every client is a risk. Every time you walk into court it's a risk. It's all risk, isn't it? What else is there but endless risk? [A solo practice is] not for the faint-hearted."

Q: What legal or practice skills were you least prepared for?
"Motion practice. Motions. Motions. Motions. The heart of family court."

Q: Describe your most difficult client experience, and what you learned?
"The worst clients are always the ones your gut tells you to run from at the start . . . but you don't listen."

Q: What financial issues loom in the first year?
"Malpractice insurance, health insurance, student loans . . . and [making sure to] pay yourself."

Q: What business skills are essential for a solo?
"QuickBooks."

Q: Can you solo on a shoestring budget?
"It all depends on how you define shoestring. There are some things you can't skimp on:

a basic office set-up, supplies, malpractice insurance, an accountant (at least at tax time), and money for networking/marketing events. Things you CAN skimp on: an expensive office, and an assistant or paralegal to start out."

Q: What's the biggest goof you ever made, and how was it resolved?
"I am constantly revising my retainer agreements to try to eliminate problems that rise from not being clear enough with clients about what happens when 'things come up'. Live and learn."

Q: What do you like/dislike about the autonomy of being a solo?
"I love the autonomy [of solo practice] because I hate being told what to do, and I hate having to compromise my values or my ideals. [The downside of autonomy] is that sometimes I get guilted into taking a smaller [fee] than I should from a client, and I wish I had someone around who would [point that out]. I am learning to let go of that guilt, and just do what I need to do for my business."

Q: What role do people skills play in a solo's success?
"They're crucial. I occasionally meet other lawyers whose personalities leave something to be desired, and I know they would never make it as a solo. I feel like telling them they should thank their lucky stars they have the partners and paralegals to do it all for them."

Q: Does social media play a role in your practice?
"Facebook has been a major marketing tool and LinkedIn a minor one. And while I don't tweet often, I do tweet."

Q: What are some of the biggest challenges when you're The Boss?
1) "Isolation, overwork, and the fact that there's no one [but yourself] to blame. If it all falls apart, the buck stops [with you]."

Q: What would you tell new solos about marketing?
"Spend at least 50 percent of your time marketing . . . and don't just rely on the Internet. Go out and meet people; shake hands; hand out cards; go to networking events; go to charity events. Make sure every person you meet knows what you do and how to reach you."

Q: Where do you see the practice of law, and solo'ing, headed?
"I think that solos and small firms are going to blossom, picking up where some of the antiquated big firms are losing clients."

Q: Linda, what are your thoughts about job security? "Who has job security? I think I have more than most; at least I know I won't fire myself!"

MITCHELL MATORIN

Education: Duke University School of Law; Class
of 1993

Resume: Practicing law for 18 years

Solo practice: Four years

Practice specialties: Business litigation, IP
litigation, Appellate practice

Q: Why did you decide to solo?

"I practiced for 18 years, three-and-a-half at the
Department of Justice, and the remainder at two
large law firms. I wasn't happy with my career
choice after leaving DOJ. Not because there was
anything wrong with my firms; they were both
good places with smart, caring people, and
interesting work. I just wasn't cut out for the
big law firm culture. So, I cast about for years,
trying to figure out what else I could do. I had
never seriously considered [solo'ing], but after
scratching out some calculations on a pad of
paper, multiplying hourly rate by billable hours,
I realized that even if I didn't have a ton of work
at first, the numbers were actually very favorable.
So I leaped."

**Q: Now, four years later, how do
you feel about the decision?**

"No regrets at all."

Q: What's your plan B if things don't work out?

"Plan B? See Plan A."

Q: What about job security?

"You don't have much job security in a law firm
anyway, as the last few years have demonstrated
quite nicely. My job security now lies in my ability
to get the job done, and to have clients who think
highly of me, and respect what I've done
for them."

**Q: What are your sharpest memories
of starting out?**

"[When I started my firm], I didn't have much in
the way of savings, and I financed my practice by
drawing on my home equity line of credit. We lived
frugally for a few months; not nearly as frugally
as we could have or should have, but frugally
enough."

**Q: How did you create a revenue
stream in the beginning?**

"My practice was, and still is, heavily dependent
on referrals from other solo attorneys, and from
my old firm (a word of advice: never burn bridges).
With a litigation practice, it only takes one or two
cases to get a reasonably consistent and lasting
revenue stream. If I had a transactional practice or
a family-oriented practice where I had to hustle for
each client and each client offered only a discrete
revenue potential, things would have been far
more difficult for me."

Q: What sacrifices did you make to solo?

"The biggest 'sacrifice' has been of perceived
prestige. Like most law students, I was
indoctrinated [to believe] that success is
measured by the name of your firm and the size
of your paycheck. It took some time to get my
mind around the idea that it might not be that way,
and the number of big firm attorneys who have
told me that they envy me—or who have sought
me out to talk about my career path—never
ceases to amaze me."

**Q: What do you like/dislike about
the autonomy of solo practice?**

"I love not having to answer to anybody other
than my client (and the Court), but I miss the
ability to walk next door and bend somebody's
ear on an issue."

Q: How do you balance parenting with a solo practice?

"It's more than a little unnerving not having a guaranteed monthly income when you have kids who insist on eating every day, [and on top of that] a mortgage and living expenses. [As a solo], it's great to be able to control my own schedule— somewhat—and to be able to guarantee that I can attend certain things. On the other hand, I also feel compelled to work late because everything depends on me, with the unfortunate result that I'm usually not home for dinner. Somewhere, there's a happy medium . . . but I haven't found it yet."

Q: Describe your most difficult client experience, and what you learned?

"My worst client was my first. It was a non-litigation matter, and I had offered him a choice of hourly or fixed fee and he chose fixed. The client turned out to be extremely demanding and required constant hand-holding, and did a lot of things on his own that made things unnecessarily complex. I finally lost my patience and told him he should find another attorney. Lesson learned: sometimes you have to fire a client to stay in business . . . and it's OK to do that."

Q: What was your biggest goof?

"Letting a client accrue a huge outstanding balance on a litigation matter that took a tremendous amount of my time (and many all-nighters). I let the empathy I felt for the client, who had to defend against a full-blown lawsuit over a dispute that easily should have settled, get in the way of good business sense. Although empathy is a good thing, when it comes to running a solo practice it has to be backed up with a somewhat cold-hearted view of the bottom line."

Q: How important is it to prepare a business plan?

"Whether or not to write a business plan, probably depends on experience level and practice area. For me, it was not important at all. At least, I didn't have one, and I wouldn't know how to write one. It's possible, though, that I might be vastly more wealthy and nearing financial security if I had had a business plan. I guess ignorance is bliss."

Q: Can you solo fresh from law school?

"If you have to [solo without previous legal experience], or if you have always felt that this is what you want to do, then go for it. But if you have the option of working in a firm for a few years, do it instead. You'll see how things are really done, and that will translate into self-confidence that you actually can do it."

Q: How would advise new solos about marketing?

"Network with other attorneys. Go out of your way to be helpful, and to go beyond the expected when somebody asks for advice. Join the ABA's Solosez listserv and actively participate and show your experience and willingness to help. And always be available for brainstorming with other attorneys. Get a good Web site; it doesn't have to be expensive, but it does have to be professional, informative, and most of all, it has to exist."

Q: Your advice to new solos about malpractice insurance?

"Get it. You've got enough on your mind without worrying about [a malpractice claim]. The [insurance] probably isn't as expensive as you think for a new attorney, and it will give you real peace of mind."

Q: Mitchell, where do you see the practice of law, and solo practice, headed?

"Big firm layoffs and increasing client cost pressure have opened up new opportunities for solos and small firms to take a piece of the work that always went to the big firms by default. [For this reason], I think the last few years have been transformative for the solo/small firm practice. I'm fairly hopeful about the future of solo/small firm practice generally, and about my own prospects specifically."

KARA O'DONNELL

Education: University of Miami; Class of 1995
Resume: Practicing law for 14 years
Solo practice: One year
Practice specialties: Bankruptcy, family law, civil

Q: Why did you decide to solo?

"After buying my first home only three months before, I was suddenly laid off. After a few months of no job prospects, I decided to start my bankruptcy law practice."

Q: What was the reaction among your colleagues?

"Many were surprised. Give up a weekly paycheck and health insurance? How dare I rock the boat! But the time was right to start my firm, so I chose to take the risk rather than to look for another uninspired job with a paycheck and a few benefits."

Q: What are your sharpest memories of starting out?

"[I remember] the ups and downs: having many new prospects call in a single day, and then have no one call for a week or two. I also remember working late nights to file bankruptcy cases, and then realizing happily that I could sleep late the next morning. After all I was a solo! [What I failed to consider] is that bankruptcy court usually calls at 8:30 a.m.! Now, I work into the wee hours only if I can answer calls in a coherent fashion at 8:00 the next morning."

Q: How do you handle the risks associated with solo practice?

"I [used to have] high anxiety whenever my firm's bank account was low. It was scary wondering what would happen month-to-month. After only nine months of being a solo, though, that anxiety is rarely an issue. [But] the other risk involves being able to do the legal task in a professional

manner without the benefit of another attorney "down the hall" to bounce questions off. The only solution? Read . . . research . . . read more. Repeat."

Q: What are the biggest challenges when you're The Boss?
Making money. Getting clients. Knowing your field of law."

Q: What do you do to make sure your business maintains profitability?
Keep all expenditures low, and don't spend your money unless you really need to."

Q: What did you sacrifice to solo?
"I can't go to restaurants like I used to, and my hair stylist has forgotten my name. But business is improving . . . slowly. It takes a while to develop that happy client base that will refer you to new clients. It's been nine months and I just got my first one of those yesterday."

Q: What are some of a solo's frustrations?
"I'm constantly rattling my brain, wondering how to get more clients. Where are they . . . why do they go to Attorney X . . . how does Attorney X have such a huge caseload? It's sleep-depriving."

Q: Describe your most difficult client experience, and what you learned?
"I have had clients that lie to you or conveniently forget to tell you something. I have since learned to ask anything and everything, and I watch them closely. It's a skill I learned conducting depositions for years in auto injury litigation. A facial expression can tell me there's more to the story, and I have to keep probing. My favorite client has come to my house and helped with drywall. Who wouldn't love that?"

Q: How important are people skills in a solo practice?
"An attorney's personality can be the difference between a potential client wanting to come in to sign up, and wanting to call a few other places. In general, clients like that I care about their problem, and take (a lot of) time to talk to them even on the first call."

Q: What role does networking play in a solo's success?
"A prospective solo should consider what kind of network they have available, and how they can make use of it. I started soloing in a community where I have lived for many years. I have many contacts through my extended family, my old work, my kids' school and activities, my hobbies, and my husband's work, etc. I use these contacts all the time. I couldn't imagine being successful without having this network. I don't think I would be as successful if I just opened shop in some random area."

Q: What role do mentors or contacts play in your practice?
"I wish I had more, but so many other attorneys are too busy to mentor."

Q: What do you like/dislike about the autonomy of solo'ing?
"I miss having co-workers. Sometimes I feel like the Tom Hanks character [in the movie Castaway], talking to a volleyball when he was marooned on an island in the Pacific."

Q: What's your impression of social media as a marketing tool?
"Social media makes practicing more affordable in that you can get your message out faster and cheaper than old fashioned print ads and articles."

Q: What would you tell a roomful of new law grads about solo'ing? "Have a slush fund for the first two to three months. Do doc review if you have nothing in your bank account; intern if you have to. Just get experience, and always be hungry for the next opportunity. You never know where it will lie. Just don't quit even when business gets slow . . . even if it is slow for two months! And keep reading and educating yourself. There is a wealth of information on the listservs [e.g., Solosez], where much more experienced solos are posting their opinions and helpful hints."

Q: Your advice to new lawyers about malpractice insurance? "Buy it. In large amounts."

Q: Kara, what does the future hold for solo practice? "Like all businesses, the truly hungry [solos] will be in it for the long haul, and the meek will move into paycheck jobs. I have hope for me; if I don't, who will?"

PAUL "WOODY" SCOTT
Education: Louisiana State University;
    Class of 2008
Resume: Practicing law for 2 years; previously,
    a law firm associate
Solo practice: 1 $1/2$ years
Practice specialties: Immigration, Criminal Defense

Q: Why did you decide to solo?
"I have always wanted to start a business and work for myself. Back in law school, I clerked for big firms and small firms, but I liked the small firm lifestyle better. Once, I clerked for a solo practitioner, and she decided to spend a few weeks in Ecuador and had work sent to her via email. That really appealed to me."

Q: What about job security?
"When I put in my last two weeks at my former law firm, I was paralyzed by nervousness about going out on my own. It lasted all of two days. Then one day I just snapped out of it and realized that the only job security out there is the job security that I create for myself. Once I started working in my own office I actually felt a sense of empowerment that I was creating my own job, and that no one was going to be able to take it away from me."

Q: How did you bring in a stream of revenue in the beginning?
"Contract work for a local non-profit agency. It was my only guaranteed income. It didn't pay much, but I enjoyed the work and it has lead to a lot of referral sources."

Q: What role does a spouse/partner play in a solo's success?
"My wife has been and still is an amazing pillar of support for me. More than anyone, she encouraged me to go out on my own . . . and kept

encouraging me when I got cold feet. She also is a part-time legal assistant, helping me around the office when I fall behind or just need help."

Q: Given what you've learned, would you still solo? "Absolutely. I love getting up every day to go to the office. I like being able to choose my cases and how I am going to handle them. It is certainly a sacrifice to go solo, but the sacrifice will pay off in dividends if done right."

Q: What's your Plan B if things don't work out? "I've never had a Plan B. But if I do see [things] aren't working out, I'll work on one. Until then, all my time, energy, and focus is going into Plan A."

Q: Can you solo on a shoestring budget? "The number one reason new businesses fail is . . . undercapitalization. I think most lawyers start off their firms on a shoestring, which makes a business plan even more important. [Before you solo], there should be a definite plan that lays out expenses and a few definite referral sources in place. The less money you have to start, the stricter your budget needs to be."

Q: What role do mentors play? "Mentors have been a huge part of my practice. Many times I come to a situation where I don't quite know the next step, or how to proceed in a case. After I have done as much research as I can, I will call a mentor or a colleague who practices in that area and bounce the idea off of them. I find that lawyers are almost always willing to talk out a case or scenario with you. And when they call me for help, I always make sure I am available to repay the favor. If you get involved in bar associations and groups, you are bound to meet many people in the field who will be able to help you when you are stuck in a situation."

Q: How important is a business plan? "A business plan is of the utmost importance. I don't see how [a solo practice can succeed] without one. It doesn't have to be super-formal. Just a basic budget; things like how much expenditures you will be making each month, how much money you need to cover those expenses, how much you need to cover overhead, and to bring home a decent salary."

Q: What role does risk play in a solo practice? "Risk is a big factor in starting a solo practice. The goal should not be to avoid risk, but to understand, mitigate, and manage it. You have to be willing to risk your money, savings, and steady paycheck. But if you make a good business plan, and you stick to it, and you see how you are going to feed yourself, you are managing that risk. Before I started my solo practice, I spent hours and hours in front of Excel spreadsheets, figuring out how much income I would need for the practice to stay afloat, how much I needed to bring home, etc. I take the same approach with cases that I decide to take, marketing decisions, etc. There is always going to be a risk that you won't get a good return on your investment."

Q: What practice skills were you least prepared for? "Doing the books. You have to constantly stay on top of it or you lose control of your money, and not know how much you are making v. spending. Now, I save every receipt and make sure everything is entered in Quickbooks. I spend a lot of time on [accounting], because it lets me know where I'm profiting and where I'm losing money. Until you review your Quickbooks reports, you will be surprised at some of the things draining money from your firm."

Q: Should a new law grad start a solo practice?

"It is certainly possible to hang your shingle right out of law school, but it would certainly be better to get a few years of experience. Not necessarily legal experience; rather, how the inner workings of a law firm work: how to create files, how correspondence should be saved, etc. If getting a few years experience is not possible, some law school internships could definitely achieve the same goal. And if that is not possible, go to a lot of CLE's on law practice management."

Q: What would you tell new solos about marketing?

"Before starting my firm, I went to a seminar on going solo. One of the presenters—a very successful personal injury lawyer—offered a piece of marketing advice that I will never forget: 'the best marketing you can do is to respect your clients, because even a client with a small personal injury case might have a cousin, a brother, a friend, etc., who may one day have a million dollar case . . . and you want to make sure you get that referral.' This stuck with me, and is something I use in my practice today. My advice [to new solos] would be to be a people person and give EVERYONE respect. I have gotten more clients from just being present at events and being nice to people. I have given free consultations to people who did not retain me because there was nothing I could do to help them, or because they could not afford the fee. They should still be treated like they are the most important person in the office, and don't forget to give them some (many) cards on the way out! They will usually take them gladly, and they will be your biggest referral sources before you know it."

JAN TAMANINI

Education: Dickinson School of Law; Class
    of 1984

Resume: Practicing law for 26 years; previously,
    a TV news anchor/reporter, and press
    secretary for government agencies

Solo practice: Four years

Practice specialties: Business/nonprofit
    transactions, estate planning,
    government procurement

Q: Is there a solo type?

"One really important thing about being solo is disciplining yourself to do what you have to within the time you have to do it. There's no one looking over your shoulder or e-mailing you to ask how you're progressing with a matter. So if you're the type of person who needs constant poking to get work done, perhaps solo practice isn't right for you."

Q: Why did you decide to solo?

"I spent over 25 years working in state government, most of them as an attorney for several different state agencies working with contractors and grantees. I had a couple of amazing bosses, but most of them were on power trips, enjoying making their staff miserable, or who were so paralyzed that they couldn't make decisions to save their souls. About two years before I left my government job, I got my hands on as much literature as I could from the bar and the Internet. And I read a lot about marketing for small businesses, and about having a private consulting business."

Q: What did you tell your colleagues?

"Most [of them] were aware of my unhappiness with my work environment, [but they thought] I was blowing smoke and wouldn't follow through.

But [after 25+ years in government], I just couldn't stay in a safe but soul-sucking environment just for the security it provides."

Q: How did you create a revenue stream in the beginning?
"I talked with as many people as possible about what I was doing. Every social occasion, every networking event, every possible opportunity, was a chance to mention my business. I honed my 'elevator speech' so that when someone asked what I did for a living, I had a coherent, interesting answer. I asked friends for business; I asked for referrals. And I distinguished my practice from what other attorneys in the area were doing. [My advice]: keep reminding people about your value and services, and many will eventually come around. But one contact is not enough; it usually takes several 'touches' to get someone interested."

Q: How important is a business plan?
"Whether you draft a traditional, formal business plan, or spend just a few pages outlining your goals and expectations, you really should have some plan in place . . . and review it and update it regularly (say, every six months). Without one, it would be like driving across country without a map. Sure, you may eventually get to your destination, but it won't be by the most direct or effective route."

Q: What are you doing to maintain profitability?
"In addition to the standard networking, I check in with current clients, friends, and business contacts on a somewhat regular basis to ask if there's anything they might need in the way of the services that I provide . . . or if they know anyone who may be in need of my services. It's hard at first to ask directly for referrals, but it really pays dividends."

Q: Can you solo on a shoestring budget?
"Hell, yes. It's what I do every day! There are times when the money is coming in gangbusters, and other times when I wonder when I'll get new work to pay the bills. This unpredictability takes a strong stomach. But if you can get by without an ostentatious office and use the Internet and local resources to make your practice work, you really don't need to lay out the big bucks."

Q: What role does risk play in solo practice?
"It isn't that much different from those borne by other practitioners . . . with one exception: it's all on you. There's no one else to take up the slack if you have a slow period or get sick. And if one of your clients has a crisis demanding big chunks of your time, you can't just let everything else slide. The best way I've found to manage this—and it's still a struggle for me—is to make sure I give myself more time than I think I'll need to complete a client project. If something should take a few days, I'll tell the client I'll get it done in 10 days; if it should take a week, I'll tell the client two."

Q: What do you like/dislike about the autonomy of solo'ing?
"Too much online and phone contact without face time can make you a little stir crazy. The ease of having a colleague down the hall to bounce ideas around is something I miss from my earlier days. [As a solo], you have to make a point to pick up the phone and arrange a time to talk, or better yet, a time to meet in person."

Q: What marketing advice do you have for new solos? "You really have to make an effort to be involved with your business community. If you sit in a home office and wait for work to come to you, they'll be hauling your dust-covered skeleton out at the end. Maintain outside contacts with both friends and business associates; get out to networking events, volunteer with local groups (you may find great referrals from those efforts), and have lunch outside of your office on a regular basis. The isolation is something you really have to work to overcome. Also, focus on a few primary practice areas instead of trying to do everything."

Q: Any other thoughts about marketing?
"Yes, don't be afraid to ask clients or networking colleagues to pass your name along to their friends, customers, and business partners, and don't get discouraged if someone doesn't hire you immediately. It might take months, it might take years. And have your 'elevator pitch' ready and tailored to the group you're with at the time. You never know when you might run into someone who could use your help, or who may know someone else who does."

Q: Jan, what about job security?
"I have the most secure job in the world. I can't be fired. I can lose a client, but I'll always be able to find others. And I have no psychotic boss who enjoys making me feel as if I'm about to go in front of the firing squad every day. I know I have the skills and personality needed to succeed [as a solo]. To me that's more valuable than any salary."

MARK TANNEY
Education: Thomas Jefferson School of Law; Class of 1998
Resume: Practicing law for 10 years in large and midsize DC firms; previously, a professional chef for 18 years
Solo practice: 1 year
Practice specialty: Consumer bankruptcy

Q: Why did you decide to solo?
"I was laid off from a good DC law firm in June 2009 after working there for six years. At first I thought about seeking employment again with a firm or with the government. I worked up a number of resumes and applied for a few positions . . . but my heart was not in it. I could barely force myself to write another cover letter stating, yet again, how I was a 'team player', a 'self starter', and a 'problem-solver'. I knew that I wanted to go out on my own."

Q: What sacrifices did you make to solo?
"We sold our house and moved to a rented townhouse half the size. I mostly work seven days a week right now. Financially we have downsized and reined in our standard of living considerably. I have lost a fair amount of sleep."

Q: Your thoughts about job security?
"We seem to be moving away from the traditional BigLaw model. [In my opinion], working for a firm will provide little real job security as this trend continues. As a solo, I can never be fired . . . and I can't be forced to retire. If I can get [my solo practice] off the ground, my job security will actually be greater."

Q: What role does a spouse/partner
play in a solo's success?

"Starting a solo practice is such an all-consuming
process that the spouse plays a big role —positive
or negative —regardless of whether he or she
wants to. A supportive spouse will help you
through the hard times and possibly provide a
financial bridge during start up. A skeptical or
reluctant spouse can be a drain on your energy
and emotional resources. Your spouse's views
should be carefully considered before you head
down this road."

Q: Given what you've learned, would
you still solo?

"I'm having a great time doing what I'm doing. I
look forward to it every day, and I can't wait to get
to my desk in the morning. I'm not yet on solid
ground financially. But I'll always be glad I [solo'd]
no matter how it turns out."

Q: What are sharpest memories
of opening your practice?

"I'm still in my first few months of practice, so
my sharpest memories are not too far removed.
I think that I will always remember the feeling of
doing everything for the first time: creating law
firm forms and other client materials; setting
up a Web site and blog; purchasing supplies
and equipment; registering my business
with the city; opening bank accounts; joining
organizations; attending meetings, seminars and
CLE's; marketing; and continuing my study of the
substantive law. Everything is new, everything is
urgent. Each day I feel like I am completing only
half of my 'must-do' list for the day."

Q: How risky is it to start a solo practice?

"It varies. If a solo has money in the bank and
a good book of business, the risk may not be
that great; conversely, if the attorney is starting
out with a minimal budget, no client base, and
huge student loans, then the attorney will have a
much greater risk. Other factors also play into the
picture. If you are 30 years old and able to work a
full time job while you start your practice, this may
help reduce your risk. And if your spouse is willing
and able cover expenses until you get off the
ground, that, too, will help reduce your risk."

Q: Any other thoughts about risk?

"Yes, take a long look at your finances before
starting. If you have three young children, no
savings, and $1,200 in monthly student loan
payments, then starting a new law practice is
going to be tough. It's still possible, just difficult.
Beyond the financial issue, the key question goes
to motivation: the key indicator of a solo's success
is a true desire to solo. If you want solo just to get
through the downturn until the jobs come back,
it may prove difficult."

Q: How important is a business plan?

"I don't think [it] is very important. Sure, you
should take pen to paper and get a general sense
of what it will cost to open your doors, how much
income you need to bring in, how soon you need
income, etc. As a new solo, your business plan can
be as simple as this: spend as little as you can, do
everything you can do to market your business,
and do a good job. That's the plan. If you do those
things, you've done what you can to succeed."

Q: How important is it that a solo have good people skills?

"People skills are important, but I don't think it is essential that you have a super outgoing personality. When you network, just ask people about themselves and pay attention; and when you work with clients, treat them with respect, keep your promises, and stay in touch. Those are the things that matter. If you are also really friendly and outgoing, that will be a plus . . . but not essential."

Q: What business skills were you least prepared for?

"I've been a lawyer for about 10 years, but I've always worked for firms. I have no experience marketing or operating a law firm, and I was not prepared for marketing and practice management. I have been teaching myself through reading and trial and error, and I'm making good progress. But I have a long way to go."

Q: What would you tell new solos about marketing?

"My advice is spend most of your time marketing . . . especially at the beginning. Don't just attend Chamber of Commerce meetings and hand out your business card to 100 people. Find the networking methods that make sense for your practice area and do those."

Q: What would you tell new solos about malpractice insurance?

"The main risk is the cost of defense if someone brings a complaint. In Washington DC [malpractice insurance] is not required, but I have it mainly to protect my family. It's not necessarily the first priority, but I think it is probably a good idea to get insurance as soon as you can."

Q: Is there a solo type?

"The key is one's strong desire to be a solo. If you have that, you have a good chance to succeed. Beyond that, of course it helps to be tech-savvy, socially outgoing, and competent in the substantive law. But the key is your desire to be solo."

Q: Mark, what does the future hold for a solo legal practice?

"I think there's a big future for solo and small firm law. The BigLaw business model seems to be fading. [In the future], prospective clients using Internet resources will be able to solve routine legal problems on their own. But they will still need lawyers for issues they cannot resolve for themselves. Solo lawyers can succeed, but they will need to be highly sensitive to what clients actually need lawyers to do."

Solos by Choice: The Complete List of Companion Guide Contributors

DAVID ABESHOUSE

Education: Vanderbilt School of Law; Class of 1982

Resume: Practicing law for 28 years; associate in medium and small suburban law firms, and medium New York firm, partner/medium suburban firm

Solo Practice: 11 years

Practice specialties: Business litigation, arbitration, mediation (commercial and ADR), and business arbitrator and mediator

Bottom line: "There are two diametrically opposed schools of thought [about] solo'ing right out of law school. For myself, I feel it was important that before I went solo I had a good grounding in the substantive law via work experience, practice skills, and practice management."

KEVIN AFGHANI

(see page 96 for the expanded profile)

Education: Tulane School of Law; Class of 2004

Resume: Practicing law for five years; previously, an associate with Sonnenschein, Nath, Rosenthal

Solo practice: Two years

Practice specialty: Patent law

Bottom line: "I gave up a BigLaw salary and a regular paycheck for no guaranteed income at no guaranteed time. [The sacrifice] was worth every penny."

UBONG AKPAN

Education: American University; Class of 2003

Resume: Practicing law for seven years; previously, an associate at two Biglaw firms and a judicial clerk at appellate court

Solo/small firm practice: 1 year

Practice specialties: Immigration, personal injury, family law, appellate practice

Bottom line: "A business plan is important, but if you start your solo practice without one

make sure you have a set of goals you work towards."

DEAN N. ALTERMAN

Education: Lewis & Clark Law School; Class of 1989

Resume: Small firm for nine years, large firm for eight years; went solo in 2006, gradually expanding to become a partner in a seven-lawyer firm

Practice areas: Commercial and investment real estate, corporate, and land use

Bottom line: "I worked for two years on my business plan before I opened my practice, and I am very glad I did. Without it, I think it would have taken four to six months to turn a profit; with the plan, I made a profit within two months after opening and in every month since."

BRIAN M. ANNINO

Education: University of Connecticut; Class of 2003

Resume: Practicing law for five years; previously, corporate counsel, associate

Solo practice: Two years

Practice specialties: Business law, estate planning, probate, real estate law

Bottom line: "Never underestimate the power of face-to-face networking."

GINA BONGIOVI

(see page 98 for the expanded profile)

Education: University of Nevada/Las Vegas, JD/MBA; Class of 2007

Solo practice: Practicing law for two years

Practice specialty: Part-time general counsel for small businesses

Bottom line: "Be honest with yourself; not everyone is cut out to have their own practice.

You'll be miserable if you try to be a business owner when you might be happiest as an employee."

LAEL BROWN

Education: McGeorge School of Law; Class of 2009

Resume: Practicing law for one year; previously, a university lab administrator

Solo practice: One year

Practice specialties: Probate and trust administration, real estate and elder law, general civil litigation

Bottom line: "As a solo, the practice of law is so much more meaningful [because] I get to interact and help my clients directly without worrying about meeting my billing quota."

BRUCE CAMERON

(see page 100 for the expanded profile)

Education: Hamline University School of Law; Class of 2007

Resume: Practicing law for three years; previously, a research scientist

Solo practice: Three years

Practice specialty: Collaborative family law, probate, and real estate work

Bottom line: "Going solo means spending large amounts of time and money in a venture with no defined return, and with odds that are undefined, unpredictable, and continuously variable! It's an intricate dance with risk . . . but NOT a gamble."

GABRIEL CHEONG

Education: Northeastern University School of Law; Class of 2007

Resume: Practicing law for four years.

Solo practice: Four years

Practice specialty: Family law, wills, trusts, prenuptial agreements

Bottom line: "As a solo, I wake up loving what I do every day. I look forward to Fridays as much as Mondays."

TONYA COLES

Education: Capital University Law School; Class of 2006

Resume: Practicing law for four years

Solo practice: Four years

Practice specialties: Estate planning, probate, elder law

Bottom line: "Good people skills are a must. You must make clients comfortable with you so that they retain you and send referrals to you."

THOMAS J. CRANE

Education: Tulane University; Class of 1983

Resume: Practicing law for 24 years, interspersed with active duty with the US Army including one tour in Iraq.

Solo practice: 14 years

Practice specialties: Employment law, general litigation

Bottom line: "The best part [of being solo] is that I cannot be fired. I've been caught up in those office politics things and [solo'ing] is much better. My success depends on no one but me."

CAILIE A. CURRIN

Education: Albany Law School, Class of 1988

Resume: Practicing law for 21 years; previously, senior attorney for state agency, law firm partner, senior compliance attorney, principal

Solo practice: Three years

Practice specialty: Insurance regulatory/ compliance

Bottom line: "I do not have a Plan B. This is my passion, and I plan to [solo] for the rest of my working career."

MARK DEL BIANCO

Education: Yale School of Law; Class of 1980

Resume: Practicing law for 31 years; previously, US Department of Justice, and small and large firm practice, including Skadden Arps/ Washington DC

Solo practice: Seven years

Practice specialties: Communications and Internet

Bottom line: "Getting good clients is all about networks; hometown, college, law school, government, firm, etc. Unless you have two or three good, separate networks, making it as a solo is very difficult."

BRUCE L. DORNER

Education: New England School of Law; Class of 1977

Resume: Practicing law for 33 years

Solo practice: About 31 years

Practice specialties: General practice emphasizing transactions and problem-resolution including Collaborative Law

Bottom line: "To solo, you need the guts to trust yourself, the desire to get up every day and hustle, and the willingness to admit that you don't know as much as you thought you did."

HERBERT ALAN DUBIN

Education: Brooklyn Law School; Class of 1964

Resume: Practicing law for 46 years; previously, prosecutor with the Interstate Commerce Commission & Civil Aeronautics Board; associate then partner in a transportation law firm in

Washington DC; partner in DC office of multi-city firm.

Solo practice: About 23 years

Practice specialties: Transportation law, commercial / business civil litigation, personal injury, domestic, criminal defense, and

attorney discipline defense

Bottom line: "Overhead and cash flow: those are the biggest financial issues that can sink a solo at any time."

TRACI D. ELLIS

Education: Ohio State University; Class of 1990

Resume: Practicing law for 20 years; previously, midsize firm, in-house at Fortune 500 company, and small privately held company

Solo practice: Four years.

Practice specialties: General business; primarily for women entrepreneurs

Bottom line: "The best marketing I've ever done has been to write articles for a publication read by my target clients. It's free publicity, and I always get calls. I suggest that solos find those publications (relevant to their practice) and get published. It's free marketing . . . and it works."

DENNIS ESFORD

Education: Chicago/Kent School of Law; Class of 2003

Resume: Practicing law for eight years; previously, a contract lawyer in large firm litigations

Solo Practice: Five years

Practice specialties: Civil litigation, including contract, business torts and non-patent IP.

Bottom line: "I remember worrying that my contract assignments would suddenly end with no replacement in sight. But a week after my first assignment, I had another . . . and I have been working continuously ever since."

ERIC P. GANCI

Education: Thomas Jefferson School of Law; Class of 2008

Solo practice: One year

Practice specialty: DUI defense

Bottom line: "Don't put your practice on a credit card, or borrow from friends/relatives. Who needs that stress?"

VARAND GOURJIAN

Education: UCLA School of Law; Class of 1999

Resume: Practicing law 11 years

Solo Practice: Five years

Practice specialties: Business transactions and litigation, real estate transactions, bankruptcy

Bottom line: "I didn't know much about solo practice before I began, except that everyone with whom I spoke who had taken the plunge said they were much happier and never return to a large firm."

LYNDA L. HINKLE

(see page 103 for the expanded profile)

Education: Rutgers University/Camden; Class of 2009

Resume: Practicing law for nearly two years; previously, teacher, writer, Congressional aide

Solo practice: ⋯⋯≥1 year

Practice specialties: Family, wills/estates, and small business

Bottom line: "The worst clients are always the ones your gut tells you to run from at the start . . . but you don't listen."

WALTER D. JAMES III

Education: University of Nebraska School of Law; Class of 1987

Resume: Practicing law for 24 years; previously, large firm practice as an associate and partner

Solo Practice: Seven years

Practice specialties: Environmental law

Bottom line: "Keep marketing, and never ever rest on your laurels."

JENNY JELTES

Education: Wayne State University; Class of 2006

Resume: Practicing law for four years; previously, a law firm associate

Solo practice: One year

Practice specialties: Domestic relations, general civil litigation

Bottom line: "My goal is to eventually have my practice become profitable enough so I no longer need to do boring contract document review work!"

MATTHEW G. KAISER

Education: Georgetown University; Class of 2002

Resume: Practicing law for eight years; previously, assistant federal public defender, and associate for Biglaw and Mid-size firms

Solo practice: Two years

Practice specialties: Federal criminal defense, plaintiff personal injury

Bottom line: "If you've got kids, I don't know how you could solo without a seriously supportive spouse. It's a lot of time away from the family and I just couldn't do it without a supportive partner."

NINA KALLEN

Education: Northeastern University; Class of 1994

Resume: Practicing law for 15 years; previously, judicial clerkship, six years with insurance defense practices

Solo practice: Nine years

Practice specialties: Brief writing for other lawyers on a subcontract basis; insurance coverage; civil litigation

Bottom line: "If you try [solo'ing] but you don't like it . . . move on. Nothing has to be forever."

STEPHANIE KIMBRO

Education: University of Dayton School of Law; Class of 2003

Resume: Practicing law for eight years, including two years in a small firm

Solo practice: Nearly five years (virtual law office)

Practice specialties: Estate planning, small business set-up, unbundling legal services

Bottom line: "I consider myself an entrepreneur, and I enjoy controlling the structure of my practice, scheduling my own days, and not being held back by the conventional structures of a traditional law practice."

LAURA S. MANN

Education: Hofstra University; Class of 1996

Resume: Practicing law 14 years, including 10 years in legal services

Solo practice: 3 1/2 years

Practice specialties: General practice with a current focus on family law, bankruptcy, and civil litigation

Bottom line: "As a single mother, I found starting and having my own practice to be very tough, very challenging . . . very scary. The fear of not knowing when or if a paying client will walk through the doors can be overwhelming at times. . . . "

MARC W. MATHENY

Education: Indiana University/Indianapolis School of Law; Class of 1980

Solo practice: 30 years

Practice specialties: Civil litigation, probate litigation, family law

Bottom line: "The struggles of solo practice are no worse or better than the struggles of any other legal practice . . . just different. But if a regular paycheck is a must, then solo practice is not for you."

MITCHELL J. MATORIN

(see page 105 for the expanded profile)

Education: Duke University School of Law; Class of 1993

Resume: Practicing law for 18 years

Solo practice: Four years

Practice specialties: Business litigation, IP litigation, Appellate practice

Bottom line: "Like most law students, I was indoctrinated that success is measured by the name of your firm and the size of your paycheck. It took some time to get my mind around the idea that it might not be so."

ABBE W. MCCLANE

Education: Western New England College School of Law; Class of 2003

Resume: Practicing law for seven years

Solo practice: Seven years

Practice specialties: General practice with emphasis on real estate, probate, elder law

Bottom line: "I enjoy the freedom of running my business as I decide, but it would be nice to have another attorney close by with whom to discuss cases and situations."

SARAH FERN MEIL

Education: Yale University (BA; Class of 2000), Columbia Law School; Class of 2003

Resume: Practicing law for eight years.

Solo practice: Five years

Practice specialty: Employee rights

Bottom line: "[Before I solo'd] I knew enough to know that I didn't know much. But I also knew that thousands of lawyers all over the country were practicing as solos, and they were making it work somehow."

MICHAEL MOEBES

Education: Georgia State University; Class of 2003

Resume: Practicing law for seven years; previously, associate of midsize firm of 90 lawyers, and as in-house counsel

Solo practice: Two years

Practice specialty: Worker's comp

Bottom line: "One of the reasons I decided to solo was to have the flexibility to have dinner with the family most every night, and pull out the MacBook after the children went to bed. When I was at a defense firm, I missed a lot of dinners and bedtimes."

JEFFREY G. NEU

Education: Rutgers University/Camden; Class of 2006

Resume: Practicing law for nearly four years; previously, law firm associate, software development

Solo practice: 3 years

Practice specialties: Technology contracting, M&A, IP, licensing, corporate

Bottom line: "[For solos], people skills are among the most important. Managing relationships and expectations will determine if you are successful or not in a solo practice."

ADAM NEUFER

Education: Golden Gate University School of Law, Class of 2009

Resume: Practicing law for 1 year

Solo practice: Seven months

Practice specialties: Divorce & family law

Bottom line: "A lot of people think that going solo means a better work schedule because you're in charge. But you [often] end up working longer and harder than you would at a firm."

KARA O'DONNELL

(see page 107 for the expanded profile)

Education: University of Miami; Class of 1995

Resume: Practicing law for 14 years

Solo practice: One year

Practice specialties: Bankruptcy, family law, civil

Bottom line: "As a solo, I miss having co-workers. Sometimes I feel like the Tom Hanks character [in Castaway], talking to the volleyball when he was marooned in the Pacific."

JENEE OLIVER

Education: Duquesne University; Class of 2005

Solo practice: Practicing law for six years

Practice specialties: Criminal, civil rights, general practice

Bottom line: "Don't solo unless your heart is in it. But if you do, get a mentor who is no more than 10 years out of law school. They can give you relevant, helpful advice."

BRIAN T. PEDIGO

Education: Whittier Law School; Class of 2007

Solo practice: Started a law office in June 2008 as principle attorney

Practice specialties: Consumer bankruptcy, personal injury, and consumer protection

Bottom line: "I've always wanted to be my own boss. After working under management and a boss for several years, I knew I would thrive best as my own boss . . . making the tough decisions and obtaining the results using my own initiative and skills."

D. JILL PUGH

Education: Northwestern School of Law; Class of 1994

Resume: Practicing law for 17 years

Solo Practice: 13 years

Practice areas: Employment law; primarily representing employees and also small businesses

Bottom line: "Risk and solo practice are synonymous. As rewarding as it is, solo practice is incredibly unpredictable and inherently risky. You bear the brunt of bad court decisions (especially in a contingency fee practice), and you bear the risk of clients who fail to pay."

BRIAN RABAL

Education: Thomas M. Cooley Law School; Class of 2005

Resume: Practicing law for six years

Solo practice: Three years

Practice specialties: Family law, criminal, and civil litigation

Bottom line: "[Marketing advice]? Join civil, social and fraternal organizations, and shake hands with as many people as you can."

PAUL "WOODY" SCOTT

(see page 109 for the expanded profile)

Education: Louisiana State University; Class of 2008

Resume: Practicing law for 2 years; previously, a law firm associate

Solo practice: 1 1/2 years

Practice specialties: Immigration, Criminal Defense

Bottom line: "People of all personalities are solo attorneys. [But if there is a solo type], it is the person who wants to run a business, and to live a happy life that he [or she] has some control over."

JAN M. TAMANINI

(see page 111 for the expanded profile)

Education: Dickinson School of Law; Class of 1984

Resume: Practicing law for 26 years; previously, a TV news anchor/reporter, and press secretary for government agencies

Solo practice: Three years

Practice specialties: Business/nonprofit transactions, estate planning, government procurement

Bottom line: "You can't afford to isolate yourself; make an effort to be involved with your business community. If you sit in a home office and wait for work to come to you, they'll be hauling your dust-covered skeleton out at the end."

MARK TANNEY

(see page 113 for the expanded profile)

Education: Thomas Jefferson School of Law; Class of 1998

Resume: Practicing law for 10 years in large and midsize DC firms; previously, a professional chef for 18 years

Solo practice: 1 year

Practice specialty: Consumer bankruptcy

Bottom line: "As a solo, I can never be fired . . . and I can't be forced to retire. If I can get [my practice] off the ground, my job security will actually be greater."

SARAH WHITE

Education: University of Tennessee; Class of 2002

Resume: Practicing law for three years with a firm and non-profit

Solo practice: Since 2007

Practice specialty: Trusts & estates

Bottom line: "I didn't create a formal business plan before beginning. But several months ago, I did make a marketing plan for the year. It's been VERY helpful in keeping me motivated about marketing."

SCOTT WOLFE

Education: Loyola University/New Orleans College of Law; Class of 2005

Resume: Practicing law for five years.

Solo: Five years

Practice specialties: Construction law

Bottom line: "I wanted to solo for the usual reasons: the ability to make my own schedule, the power of controlling my job security and destiny, the benefit of not having a promotional ceiling, and the rewards of being in business for yourself."

SPENCER YOUNG

Education: Golden Gate University School of Law, JD/MBA; Class of 2004

Resume: Practicing law for five years; previously, associate in small firms, and advisor to 501c3 nonprofit for four years

Solo practice: Five years

Practice specialties: Labor and employment, general litigation, estate planning, and personal injury

Bottom line: "The worst client is the one who comes to you with a crisis, steals your heart and you agree to help them for a small down payment with the rest coming later . . . and then you don't get paid."

APPENDIX
The Case for Solo Practice

Argument #1. Autonomy

Argument #2. Practical Experience

Argument #3. To Feel Like a Lawyer

Argument #4. Flexibility

Argument #5. To Own Not Loan Your Talent

Argument #6. Opportunity to Innovate

Argument #7. Career Satisfaction

Introduction

Our profession is regularly bombarded with negatives about solo practice, whether it is derogatory comments by large-firm lawyers or the legal media's spotlight on the ethical foibles of a few solos,. Even in a depressed economy where graduates' options are limited, soloing ranks below document-review or working in law-related positions (in publishing, finance or insurance) where a JD is helpful but not required. Rarely, do you hear why you might actually want to start your own law firm. In fact, solo practice remains one of the best-kept secrets of the legal profession because no one bothers to make a strong case in its defense. Until now.

In this section you'll find seven powerful arguments for starting your own firm:

1. Argument: Autonomy

WHEN I ASK SOLOS to identify the strongest reasons for starting their own practice, the one at the top of nearly everyone's list is . . . autonomy. It doesn't surprise me. In contrast to other professions, a law practice, by its very nature, demands deference: as lawyers, we serve clients, we're bound by precedent, we're constricted by a code of professional ethics. So, when you add such factors as the bureaucracy of a law firm or government practice . . . and firm hierarchy and the rigidity of a partnership track . . . and the ego-driven tendency of many lawyers to want to do things "my way," it's only natural that some lawyers crave the freedom that comes with solo'ing:

Freedom to choose cases—Above all, starting a practice liberates lawyers from the overbearing bureaucracy of practicing law in any kind of a large entity, be it a big firm, inside a corporation, or at a government agency. Within these organizations, most lawyers have no control over the cases they're assigned, and usually the younger or less-favored attorneys wind up either with the duds or more mundane tasks within a matter. Associates don't get much relief even when they take the initiative to drum up their own clients. Even when an associate gets a nibble from a potential client, he or she still needs to discuss the prospect with a supervisor or write up a proposal to a committee to justify taking on the client. And many times, firms turn away the types of clients that younger associates attract, either because the clients can't afford the firm fees, or they create a conflict with the firm's larger, institutional clients.

By contrast, solos don't have this problem. Solos can pick exactly the types of cases they want to handle, and develop their very own strategy to handle them. And at the end of the day, even though lawyers with their own practice may need to consult with their partners, or decide to seek guidance from a more experienced lawyer in making decisions about the merits of a case or pursuing a particular strategy, the decision to accept a case is theirs alone.

Not only does autonomy eliminate frustration and sense of powerlessness, it also gives solos an edge over their large-firm counterparts. Solos run their own ship, and they're the best situated to act quickly when a novel or new matter crosses their path. And because most successful solos have a propensity for risk, they're also not scared off by the prospect of taking a case that involves an area of law with which they have little or no experience. Contrast the solo mentality to that of a large firm, where a new client matter involving a unique or complicated legal question of first impression would require an endless litany of conflict tests, committee meetings, and preliminary (but still exhaustive) associate research before the firm would make a decision on whether to accept the case. By that time, the client would probably have sought other counsel.

In just one example, small-firm lawyer Tom Goldstein, who specializes in Supreme Court litigation, beat out several other large firms to snag a compelling death penalty matter. Why? Goldstein was able to decide to accept the case after consulting with his law partner, who happened to be his wife. In fact, Goldstein was already on a plane to Tennessee to meet the client while the large firms were still deliberating over whether to accept the matter. (Note: Goldstein has since moved to a large firm, where he serves as partner while his wife continues to operate their former practice with another lawyer.)

Lawyers in solo practice can also structure a firm that's conducive to the types of cases they want to take on. For example, one lawyer I know started his own firm after he grew tired of his BigLaw employer turning down potentially

precedent-setting appellate matters that he brought to the practice because the prospective clients couldn't afford the firm's hourly rates. As a solo, the lawyer opened an office in a suburban location closer to his home, and invested in the right combination of hardware and software that he could manage most administrative tasks without a full-time assistant. As a result, he was able to take on cases that his former firm declined as unprofitable. Even more satisfying, he's earning more money than he ever did at the firm.

There's also the experience of North Carolina solo Stephanie Kimbro, who started one of the first virtual law practices, i.e., an entirely Internet-based law firm. As a young associate, Kimbro noticed that her firm frequently turned away small transactional matters because they weren't cost-effective. So after her daughter was born, Kimbro and her husband created an online system that enabled Kimbro to work with clients exclusively online and streamline the workflow with forms. The increased efficiencies allowed Kimbro to economically serve the smaller clients that her former firm once turned away (see Stephanie Kimbro's Virtual Practice, Lawyers USA, Nov. 5, 2007).

Freedom in handling cases—These days, most large organizations don't exactly encourage recommendations on case strategy from associates. In fact, conventional wisdom advises associates to refrain from offering suggestions about potential case theories since the partners have likely already considered them anyway. And in a tight economy, where associates fear for their jobs, there's more incentive than ever to avoid rocking the boat.

Freedom from office politics — In many ways, working for others resembles a giant rite of passage. To get ahead, you've got to feign enthusiasm over sleep-inducing research projects or contribute money to a partner's favored charity. As Stephen Harper, a former BigLaw partner writes: "… Those at the top wield power that makes or breaks young careers, and everybody knows it. Doing a superior job is important, but working for the 'right' people is outcome determinative." Solo practice liberates you from just this sort of foolish, often degrading, demonstrations of hierarchy and power, leaving you free to actually practice law not inter-office politics.

Freedom over small matters—While most solos revel in their autonomy over substantive matters, sometimes it's just the freedom to make decisions about the smallest, most trivial things that makes the biggest difference. When I started my own practice, I made a point of choosing office supplies distinct from the standard issue at my former law firm—such as choosing Post-Its in bright pink instead of corporate yellow; expensive pens not cheap ball-points; business cards with blue print-on-cream rather than black-on-white. Not necessarily because I preferred them . . . but because I could.

WITH CORPORATE CLIENTS barring entry-level associates from handling their matters, and partners hoarding work, law firms no longer provide many opportunities for new associates to gain hands-on experience. When you establish your own law firm, it's you who gets the experience. For example, if you bring a business client with you from your former firm, you—and not the partner—will negotiate and draft the company's next contract. If it's an appellate matter, it's you who writes the brief and argues the case. And when the client calls for advice—on anything from a pressing strategic decision to how to dress for a deposition—it's your advice he or she wants because there's no one else. Solo practice also gives you opportunities to gain practical experience in new fields. Author note: When I started my firm, I'd been out of law school for five years and had never set foot in a courtroom except to observe. However, my practice specialty —energy regulatory work —didn't give me opportunity for trial work since most regulatory disputes are resolved on the papers or perhaps at an administrative hearing. So, to get the court time I craved, I signed up for court-appointed criminal cases. Within six months, I had a bench trial and argued a couple of motions, and within a year had my first jury trial. I never would have had those opportunities if I remained at a law firm, especially in my practice area.

3. Argument: To Feel like a Lawyer

BACK IN THE 19TH CENTURY, Karl Marx decried the Industrial Revolution for alienating workers from the product of their labor. He argued that where once craftsmen built a product from start to finish, the assembly line had atomized the process for the sake of efficiency, robbing the working class of the satisfaction of their craft. Sound familiar? In some ways, modern American law firms resemble the assembly lines Marx so vigorously condemned. At large firms, lawyers—primarily associates—work only on portions of a case, often never speaking with a client or even being privy to the entire matter. In fact, many lawyers today feel like paper-pushers, sleep-walking through their jobs rather than being vibrant professionals with the ability to solve problems and make a difference in people's lives.

On the other hand, solo practice makes you feel like a real lawyer, the kind of lawyer you imagined you would be back in law school. And each time you introduce yourself in the courtroom or boardroom; each time you reassure a nervous client; each time you explain to prospective clients what you can do for them, you reinforce the image of yourself as an autonomous, can-do professional with the tools to solve problems, resolve disputes, and even improve the legal system. And that feeling of being a lawyer never goes away, even when you're handling such administrative tasks as photocopying your own briefs or sending out bills late at night, because those tasks aren't the central focus of your job, but merely incidental to work as a real lawyer.

4. Argument: Flexibility

MANY SOLO AND SMALL-FIRM lawyers, especially those just starting out and working full-time, may put in nearly as many hours as their large-firm colleagues. But solo practice allows you to set your own schedule, spreading out the work in a way that works best for you. For instance, suppose that your son or daughter has important after-school soccer matches that you don't want to miss. Back at BigLaw, you would probably be too embarrassed to cut out early more than once for a family event, and if you worked in government you'd have to use up personal leave. On your own, though, you can simply get an earlier start on your work day, or make up the time after the match when your kids are in bed. Sure, there will be days when you have a conference or a court hearing you can't postpone. But generally speaking, you have far more control over your own time when the law firm has your name on the door.

Moreover, when you run your own shop, you avoid many of the inefficiencies and superficialities endemic to any large employer: the practice group meetings, the sensitivity training sessions, the ceremonial lunches, and the office happy-hours that cut into the day without relieving you of deadlines or billable quotas. In addition, at large firms, face-time is paramount to success; simply being seen by your colleagues is just as important as actually getting the job done. So, if your assigned partner prefers to remain at the office until eight, you can count on staying until after eight most nights even if you'd rather arrive at dawn to get home by dinner. Then there are the non-billable demands.

Though most associates believe their salaries more than compensate for long hours at the office, the actual calculations prove otherwise. A well-known study by the Yale Law School Career Office shows that with various non-billable workday interruptions, an associate working a 60-hour week will bill only 42.5 hours, barely meeting a 2,000-hour minimum billable requirement. Spread over a 60-hour work week, (and assuming three weeks for vacation) that $160,000 salary amounts to roughly $55/hour, which doesn't seem so bad until you consider that it amounts to just 25 percent of a large firm associate's billing rate!

And for lawyers who want or need to work part-time, few if any other alternative work situations can match the flexibility of solo practice. Though lawyers choose part-time employment for many reasons, the most common reason is to enable lawyers to stay home with their children. For many years, law firms have been grappling— mostly unsuccessfully—with ways to accommodate new parents, primarily mothers, who want a part-time schedule. But at law firms, part-time often means working almost similar hours on less interesting projects at drastically reduced pay. Moreover, part-time frequently involves "work seepage", or at least an implicit understanding that a lawyer must drop everything when a case emergency comes up. As a result, some women don't take advantage of part-time programs even when firms make them available. You can't blame law firms or government organizations for not accommodating women any better. Not surprisingly, the partners give priority to their own financial well-being and the perceived needs of their clients over the desires of a handful of women asking for alternative schedules.

When you start your own firm, though, you're the boss . . . and your needs come first. You have complete freedom to design a schedule and a practice tailored to your specific family situation.

LAWYERS TOILING AWAY at firms lose a substantial portion of their earnings to firm overhead and partner profit.

By way of example, a firm might bill a second-year associate at $250 an hour, and collect $500,000 based on a 2,000-hour billable year. Of that, the associate receives only $160,000 a year, or roughly a quarter of the firm's take. Granted, the remaining $340,000 isn't all firm profit; the firm covers your benefits (i.e., retirement contributions and health insurance), training and office space. But even deducting a generous $100,000/year for these expenses leaves the firm with a quarter-million dollars in profit. By contrast, if you were to start your own firm and generate 1,000 billable hours a year—that is, 20 hours a week at an average rate of $150/hour—you would still come out roughly the same as if you had stayed at the firm, but working far fewer hours! Just as we realize the advantages of owning rather than renting a home, lawyers should think carefully about the benefits of owning versus loaning their talents.

To be sure, solo practice has its ups and downs. After all, if you don't take care to adequately diversify your practice, or if you don't market your practice with vigilance, you could find yourself without any paying clients before too long. But consider: if you choose not to solo in these tumultuous times, you might be find yourself coping with a variety of grim scenarios: getting ejected from your law firm's partnership track after five years . . . getting unceremoniously booted from the law firm when you get too old or, if you're working at a government agency, getting relegated to low-level cases when a new political appointee comes into power. What would you have to show for yourself then?

JUST AS TECHNOLOGY has transformed travel, publishing, and the media, so has it fundamentally altered the legal landscape.

As a legal futurist, Richard Susskind explains in *The End of Lawyers? Rethinking the Nature of Legal Services* (2010), what he describes as disruptive technologies are automating many routine legal tasks, thus eroding the need for high-cost lawyers. Moreover, the Internet and cloud computing applications are enabling in-house counsel to bypass large firms and to seamlessly offshore their legal work (e.g., document review, due diligence and basic research) to India. As a result, many entry-level jobs at large law firms have been slashed by half, and they are unlikely to return. Law firm positions that do remain are being restructured. Firms are creating permanent staff attorney and non-partnership track positions to serve as a permanent source of leverage for entrenched equity partners. For details, read Steven Harper's article, *Permanent Leverage*; (AmLaw Daily, Nov. 12, 2010).

Nor are solo and small firms immune to change. Many solo and small firm lawyers who started practices 20 or 30 years ago still haven't quite made it into the Internet era. Even as today's consumers are accustomed to shopping and banking online, and spending considerable time engaged in online social media, nearly half of solo and small firm practitioners lack even a rudimentary online presence [ABA Technology Report 2009]. And still other traditional solo and small firms bemoan the rise of do-it-yourself providers like LegalZoom, which they believe are cutting into their business. Yet, they are unable to come up with viable models to compete.

These transitional times offer enormous opportunities for innovative, entrepreneurial lawyers to harness technology or to develop new business models for effective and profitable delivery of legal services. Large firms, with their multiple layers of bureaucracy, simply aren't nimble enough to run with new trends, while smaller firms have too much vested in the old ways of doing business to embrace change. Solo practice is an opportunity to innovate, and is a gateway for lawyers who have the vision to lead the profession into the future and change it for the better.

MORE THAN ANY OTHER career in law, solo practice offers great personal satisfaction. Several studies confirm that solo practitioners are more content than their large firm colleagues, noting that increased autonomy partly accounts for greater levels of satisfaction. So, too, does lower overhead and control over workload, which means that solos don't need to work as many hours. [www.abajournal.com/magazine/article/pulse_of_the_legal_profession]. Finally, most solos simply feel as if their work actually makes a difference. At a large firm, or even at a government agency, lawyers are generally part of a team that collectively takes credit for victories. By contrast, a solo's victories are their own. Moreover, many solos get to see the fruits of their labor up close, whether it's the client who avoids conviction, or keeps custody of the kids, or the company secures an environmental permit or venture funding. Doing work that matters is richly rewarding and makes solo practice a more meaningful—career-satisfying —experience.

CAREER RESOURCES FOR A LIFE IN THE LAW

Solo by Choice, The Companion Guide: 34 Questions That Could Transform Your Legal Career
By Carolyn Elefant $30/134pages (2011)

⸱

Solo By Choice 2011/2012 Edition: How to Be the Lawyer You Always Wanted to Be
By Carolyn Elefant $45/316 pages (2nd Ed., 2011)

⸱

Should You Really Be a Lawyer? The Guide to Smart Career Choices Before, During & After Law School
By Deborah Schneider & Gary Belsky $25/276 pages (2nd Ed., 2010)

⸱

The View From the First Chair: What Every Trial Lawyer Really Needs to Know
By Martin L. Grayson $45 /170 pages (2009)

⸱

Lawyers at Midlife: Laying the Groundwork for the Road Ahead
By Michael Long with John Clyde & Pat Funk $35 /224 pages (2008)

⸱

What Can You Do With a Law Degree? Career Alternatives Inside, Outside & Around the Law
By Deborah Arron $30 /352 pages (5th Ed., 2004)

⸱

Should You Marry a Lawyer? A Couple's Guide to Balancing Work, Love & Ambition
By Fiona Travis, Ph.D. $19 /168 pages (2004)

⸱

Running From the Law: Why Good Lawyers Are Getting Out of the Legal Profession
By Deborah Arron $17 /192 pages (3rd Ed., 2003)

Available (with free shipping) from LawyerAvenue Press at www.LawyerAvenue.com.